NOBODY BETTER,
BETTER THAN
NOBODY

By Ian Frazier

DATING YOUR MOM

NOBODY BETTER,
BETTER THAN NOBODY

NOBODY BETTER, BETTER THAN NOBODY

IAN FRAZIER

Farrar · Straus · Giroux

NEW YORK

Library of Congress Cataloging-in-Publication Data
Frazier, Ian.
Nobody better, better than nobody.
Contents: Authentic accounts of massacres—
An angler at heart—Nobody better, better than nobody—[etc.]
I. Title.
PS3556.R363N6   1987   814'.54   87–363

Grateful acknowledgment is made to *The New Yorker*, where all
these pieces first appeared

To my grandmother

Contents

Authentic Accounts of Massacres (1979)

3

An Angler at Heart (1982)

29

Nobody Better, Better Than Nobody (1983)

77

Bear News (1985)

119

Komar and Melamid (1986)

151

NOBODY BETTER,
BETTER THAN
NOBODY

Authentic Accounts of
Massacres

*T*he town of Oberlin, Kansas, is in the northwest corner of the state, eighty-three miles east of the Kansas–Colorado state line and a hundred and seven miles west of the geographical center of the continental United States. Oberlin has a population of twenty-five hundred and a town whistle that blows five times a day—at seven in the morning, at noon, at one in the afternoon, at six in the evening, and at ten at night— and it is the county seat of Decatur County. It was named after the town of Oberlin, Ohio. In 1878, it changed its name from its original one—Westfield— because a man named John Rodehaver gave the town some land on the condition that the name be changed to that of the town he and his family had come from in Ohio. I myself am from Ohio, and so this fact, like the fact that for many years the World's Largest Vase made its home in Zanesville, Ohio, or the fact that the first concrete pavement in America was laid in Bellefontaine, Ohio, or the fact that the comedian Bob Hope owns a share in the Cleveland Indians baseball team, is probably more interesting to me than it would be to somebody from another state. Many cities and towns in Ohio are named after places in other states or other countries (Norwalk, New Philadelphia, Versailles), but it is rare to find a place named after a place in Ohio. The reason for this is probably that people who leave Ohio do not like to be reminded of their native state, but I am sure that if there were a town anywhere named New Akron or New Lorain I would not be the only Ohioan eager to visit it. The Ohio town from which Oberlin, Kansas, gets its name has a strong humanistic tradition: it was a station on the Underground Railroad, and it is well known as the home of Oberlin College, the first coeducational college in America and a college that over the years has won many international friends as a result of its participation in the Congregational missions overseas, particularly in China. The town of Oberlin, Kansas, has a strong tradition, too, but "humanistic" is not the first word I would think of to describe it. It is as if the traditions of the Ohio Oberlin were so jolted and banged up by the thousand-mile journey across the prairie that they just didn't work the same as they had before. In the second half of the nineteenth century, many Ohioans went West and, by exaggerating certain of their personality traits, found violence and fame (among them the border raider William Quantrill, scourge of Lawrence, Kansas; the abolitionist John Brown, scourge of Pottawatomie, Kansas Territory; and George Custer). Oberlin, Kansas, reminds me of a whole town that did that. From the beginning, Oberlin, Kansas, has had about it something daring, something careening, something here-goes-hope-I-don't-get-shot, to a degree that is rare even for Western towns. Big, exciting, calamitous events have come snapping down on the prairie around Oberlin like the bars of giant mousetraps, especially during the town's early years.

My favorite of all the Western museums I have ever been to is in Oberlin, and it is called the Last Indian Raid in Kansas Museum. It commemorates the biggest thing ever to happen in or near the town —a raid by a group of Cheyennes that took place on September 30 and October 1, 1878, in which about forty settlers and at least two Indians died. The museum has exhibits, paintings, and books about the Indian raid and manuscripts of firsthand accounts of the Indian raid. It also has other exhibits about the history of the area, and it occupies five buildings, one of which is a sod house. The first time I visited the museum, in 1975, I asked the curator, Mrs. Kathleen Claar, about some of the recent photographs in the Indian-raid exhibit. One of the photographs was of a survivor of the raid, Charles Janousek, who as a baby was wounded in the head, and later cared for, by the Indians, and who then was almost a hundred years old. Another was a picture of a big Indian in a T-shirt and a cowboy hat, standing with his wife and his grandson, a little boy wearing a headdress with buffalo horns. Mrs. Claar said that since about 1956 there had been a celebration at the museum on the anniversary of the Indian raid; that every year for many years a number of the survivors had come to the celebration; and that Charles Janousek was the only one left. She said that the Indian was named Little Wolf and his grandson was also named Little Wolf; that they were the grandson and the great-great-grandson of the famous Cheyenne chief who was the leader of the Indians in the raid; that they had come to the museum when they were in the area on their way to join the rodeo circuit; that descendants of the Cheyennes had come to the museum several times in the past; and that several times Cheyennes had been invited to the celebration on the anniversary of the raid.

Late in the summer of 1978, remembering that the centennial of the Last Indian Raid in Kansas was approaching, I called Mrs. Claar and asked her if they were planning a big celebration and if the Indians were coming, and she said yes, they were planning a big celebration, and forty or fifty Northern Cheyennes were going to attend. Since the idea of descendants of the Indians and descendants of the settlers sitting around and talking seemed to me like a mirror image of heaven, I made a rental-car reservation, took money

out of the bank, flew to Chicago, changed planes, flew
to Omaha (I had a long layover in Omaha, so I walked
to the city from the airport and had a few beers at the
bar of the Omaha Hilton, where a real-estate sales-
men's convention was taking place, and then I decided that I wanted to take a close look at the Missouri
River, so I got a taxi and asked the driver to take me
to the best place to look at the river, and he said he
would, and he started telling me that he was separated
from his wife and was from New York City, and then
he dropped me off at the airport and said that the airport observation deck was the best place to see the
river, but that wasn't what I had in mind at all, so I
walked along the fence around the runway, scared up
a covey of quail, climbed a levee, walked through a
field, scared up a couple rabbits, walked through some
woods, and finally got to the black-mud, smelly banks
of the Missouri—the river that drains a vast area of
the West, the river that the Niobrara, the Yellowstone, the Big Sioux, the Knife, the Milk, the Heart,
the Bad, the Cannonball, and the Teton all run into
eventually, the river that was the main way West
when the first white men came, the river that many
trappers went up to be killed by Blackfoot Indians,
the river that sometimes used to be full of drowned
buffalo, the river on which the steamboat *Far West*
brought the news on July 4, 1876, of Custer's defeat—
and then I walked back to the airport), took a plane
to McCook, Nebraska, reached McCook after stops in

Columbus, Lincoln, Grand Island, Hastings, and Kearney, picked up my rental car, drove to Oberlin, and checked in at a motel.

The whole time I was in Kansas, I never heard an adult use a swearword. A lot of people asked me if I was married, and one man asked me if I was a Christian. In the evenings, I had either pork-tenderloin sandwiches and French fries at Lindy's, a café a block up from the Indian Raid museum, or ham with mashed potatoes, gravy, noodles, rolls, string beans, three-bean salad, pickled beets, corn relish, apple pie, ice cream, and milk at the 5th Wheel, a restaurant outside of Oberlin, on Highway 36.

One evening at sunset, I went for a drive in my rented Volaré and listened to the million radio stations you can get on the Great Plains. I came over a ridge and saw the red sun sitting on the lip of the prairie and the aerodynamically shaped shadows in the washes and gullies just as a really good song ("Rocky Top") came on the radio. I passed the feedlot north of Oberlin, with its many thousands of cattle. One of every nine cows sold for beef in America in 1977 was sold to McDonald's Restaurants.

One night, I watched TV in my motel room and after all the stations signed off I went for a drive. There were few cars on the road and no lights on in town and no people anywhere except for a man at a gas station who was ignoring a man with no teeth who was telling about a sow and her piglets he had seen walking down the highway some distance to the west.

I drove on dirt roads until I couldn't see any lights, and then I got out of the car. The prairie just kept on going and going in the night, under the faraway, random stars. I felt like a drop of water on a hot plate. I did not get so far from the car, with its engine running and its headlights on, that I could not hear the radio through the closed door.

I had been in Kansas only a short time when I found out the Indians were not going to show up at the centennial celebration.

Mrs. Kathleen Claar, curator for the past twenty years of the Last Indian Raid in Kansas Museum, in her museum two days before the centennial weekend:

"The Northern Cheyennes are coming. They have made a commitment to attend, and they have chartered a bus that seats forty-nine, so that will be quite a group. It will be senior citizens and junior- and senior-high students. The older Indians will stay at the Frontier Motel, and the younger ones will camp on the museum grounds. And I just had the best news! I went out and bowled this afternoon to try and get away from all these preparations, and Rick Salem, who owns the bowling alley, told me that if the Indians want to they can bowl for free. Wasn't that nice of him?

"We're going to have all kinds of demonstrations here at the museum on Saturday, September 30. We're going to have wood carving, spinning, grain grinding, soapmaking, butter churning, glass staining, wheat weaving, bulletmaking, needlepoint, china painting, tatting—that's like macramé, only you use fine thread—and crewelwork. We're going to have a quilt that was made a hundred years ago by a ten-year-old girl, and the biggest piece of cloth in that quilt is no more than one inch square. At the high-school cafeteria, the Oberlin Music Club is sponsoring a fashion show and salad luncheon, with new fashions and also 'Fashions from the Good Ole Days,' dating back to the turn of the century. There's going to be a horse show at the Saddle Club arena, at the fairgrounds, both Saturday and Sunday. The Oberlin Commercial Club is having a mini-tractor pull at the corner of Commercial Street and Penn Avenue on Saturday afternoon (those are the little fuel-powered toy tractors, you know), and then that night the bunch from Topeka—oh, they're wild, the Starlighters Chorus—are going to put on a medicine show here at the museum. It's called *Dr. Femur's La-Ka-Ha-Na-Klee* and I'm in it—I play a madam. It's so bad it's funny. Then after that there's going to be a street dance in front of the museum, and right before the dance we're going to judge the winners in the beard-and-mustache contest. Then on Sunday there's the memorial service at the Oberlin Cemetery at one o'clock, and then Fred and Wilma Wallsmith, of the High Plains Preservation of History Commission, are going to lead a fifty-mile tour of the massacre sites along the Beaver and Sappa Creeks.

"I really don't know what the Indians are going to do. They say they want to do their dances. I guess they'll just provide music and dancing and be up and down the street here to answer questions and talk to people. I've tried to take everything out of the museum that might offend the Indians. This exhibit here used to be the bones of an Indian woman who lived supposedly about twelve hundred to two thousand years ago. I've covered that up, but I'm scared to death that some little kid is going to say, when the Indians can hear him, 'Oh, Miz Claar, where's the bones of that Indian woman that used to be here?' And I've taken the word 'ravished' out of all the descriptions of the massacre, even though the Indians did ravish at least nine women, and some of the babies that were born later were brought up in the community and you can still see the Indian blood in the families to this day. And I've kind of pushed this exhibit about Sol Rees out of the way—he was quite an Indian fighter, and he lived with the Delawares for a while, and he had a wife who was a Delaware. I don't know whether they were legally married or not. The story goes that he finally traded his Indian wife for a pony. I did an article for the Oberlin *Herald* about him once, and I had to watch what I said, because his daughter was a friend of mine. I said, 'He was as cruel and hard as the times in which he lived'—that was how I got around most of it."

A dark-skinned young man with dark hair and eyes and an embroidered white shirtfront came in. "Hello,

Mrs. Claar, my name is Jesús Epimito, and I am staying with Mr. and Mrs. Wayne Larson. I am an International Foreign Youth Exchange student from the Philippines, and I was wondering if you have anything in your museum from the Philippines."

Mrs. Claar produced some beads that she thought were from the Philippines but that turned out to be from Puerto Rico.

"Some people think this museum is only about the Indian raid, but we have things here from every period in the history of this area. I shouldn't brag on myself, but I have one of the best collections of bob wire in the state of Kansas. This is the exhibit—'The History of the Plains Told in Bob Wire.' This wire here is called Glidden's Twisted Oval. It's from the early eighteen-seventies. This piece is called Harbaugh Torn Ribbon—it's just like a ribbon of metal with little tears in it. This wire with the big square pieces of tin on it is called Briggs Obvious. It came out in 1882. It's called 'obvious' because the cattle were supposed to see it and it wouldn't cut them up."

"Oh, what funny names these Indians have. Little . . . Wolf. Dull . . . Knife," said the Filipino student, who was looking at one of the Indian-raid exhibits.

"This wire here is a get-well gift sent to me when I was in the hospital from the isle of Tahiti by a friend of mine who got it from a Dutch artist. This wire here is handmade bob wire from the white cliffs of Dover. This wire here is from Jerusalem."

Dr. R. G. Young, a chiropractor whose office is next door to the museum, came in. He was wearing a terry-cloth shirt that zipped to the throat, and had his hands in the pockets of his blue pants. "Hey, Kathleen, when're the Indians coming? Remember the time the Indians came—oh, ten years ago—and set up their tepees in the yard and wouldn't stay at the motel? They wouldn't eat at the restaurant! They brought their own food and cooked it right out there!"

"This bob wire was on the Johnny Carson show. Not this exact wire—wire like this. It's called Tyler G. Lord. It was strung on a fence and Johnny had to put a splice in it in a certain amount of time, and he was pretty good at it, too."

A farmer came in. His lips were spotted and turned back into his mouth from chewing tobacco. "We've only had sixteen-hundredths of an inch of rain in this county since the beginning of September," he said. "We had a downpour a couple of weeks ago, but then the sun came out and the wind started to blow and it evaporated quicker than it come. I hope it rains for this centennial. That would do more good than anything."

"This wire is called Hodges Parallel Rowel. See the rowel in there, like the rowel in a spur, between the two strands? This wire is called Stover Corsicana Clip. This wire is called Kennedy Barb. You can put the barbs on this wire wherever you want."

Glenn Gavin, of the Kansas Committee for the Humanities, came in. He began to talk about getting Mrs. Claar a grant, and she was not sure what she would have to do for it. "Have you had a consulting historian involved in this?" he asked.

"Let's look at this interesting mirror over here. It's made of a piece of what was left of the mirror behind a bar in Norcatur, Kansas, after Carry Nation went in and smashed the place up. The frame of the mirror is made from a piece of the molding of the bar. When we started this museum, people brought us things from every town around here."

"An overall public humanities program can coordinate specialists in pioneer history," Glenn Gavin said.

"Let's look at this desk. It's called a Wooten Desk. Its full name is Wooton's Wonderful Patent Secretary, and it was known as the King of Desks. President Ulysses S. Grant had one, John D. Rockefeller had one, and Oberlin's leading citizen at the turn of the century owned this one. His name was Otis L. Benton, and he was warm and outgoing, but his wife was definitely the first lady of the town, and she used to give command performances, like the queen. Her name was Maude. When she came back from her trip to Europe, she had this book of her impressions privately printed. It's called *Maude Abroad*. Some people thought that should be three words instead of two, with a comma after Maude.

"This is a picture of the only Negro ever to live in Oberlin. Well, he wasn't the only one. He had a wife. He lived in the town for many years and was loved and respected by all who knew him.

"This is a map of Oberlin done by a man with a wooden leg.

"These are books that were written about the Indian raid—*Cheyenne Autumn*, by Mari Sandoz, and *The Brass Command*, by Clay Fisher. *Cheyenne Autumn* was made into a movie.

"This is a fossil skeleton of a prehistoric shark which was found on the Smoky Hill River near Sharon Springs by a man who was an alcoholic and liked to look for arrowheads and fossils. Some of that arrowhead collection from forty-nine of the fifty states was his, too.

"This is a collection of buttons—shell buttons, glass buttons, buttons from Europe, all kinds of buttons—worth over three thousand dollars.

"This is an arrow recovered from the stomach of a cow belonging to James A. Gaumer after the Indian raid.

"This is a cigar made by an Oberlin woman who once worked in a cigar factory in New York City.

"This is a stuffed cobra with electrical tape around it where it broke. A serviceman who was married to a local girl gave it to the museum.

"These books—*A History of the Indians of the United States*, by Angie Debo, and *Crimsoned Prairie*, by S. L. A. Marshall—were in a house that my assistant, Esther Kump, and her husband rented to some people who had kids and the kids got into the books and shot them up. Used them for target practice."

There was a phone call for Mrs. Claar. "Maybe it's the Indians," she said.

Writings having to do with the Indian raid:

Authentic Accounts of Massacre of Indians, Rawlins County, Kansas, 1875, and Cheyenne Indian Raid in Western Kansas, September 30, 1878, a booklet compiled by George Nellans, contains a copy of the official report submitted by Second Lieutenant Austin Henely, of the 6th United States Cavalry, on an attack he led on Cheyenne Indians camped on the Sappa Creek, in Rawlins County (the county next to Decatur County, where Oberlin is). Henely says that on April 19, 1875, he took forty men and pursued a band of Indians for four days until he met up with some buffalo hunters who showed him where the Indians were. He found the camp and attacked it at daylight, and killed nineteen men (including two chiefs, a medicine man, and a brave who attempted unsuccessfully to escape with "peculiar side-long leaps") and eight women and children. He burned all the lodges, destroyed or took all the arms and ammunition, and captured all the ponies. He lost only two men himself. The booklet also contains a copy of the official report filed on October 26, 1878, by Captain William G.

Wedemeyer, of the 16th United States Infantry, on the lives lost and the property destroyed and stolen in the Indian raid in Decatur and Rawlins Counties along the Solomon, the Prairie Dog, the Beaver, and the Sappa Creeks on September 30 and October 1. The men killed were homesteaders, cowboys, Czechoslovakian immigrants, men hunting land, young men of no family and no fixed address, and a traveling preacher. The lost property was cattle, horses, mules, hogs, chickens, patent medicines, carpenter's tools, eight hundred pounds of flour, coffee, molasses, sugar, bacon, men's clothing, women's clothing, children's clothing, clocks, books, pictures, jewelry, a telegraph sounder and key, guns, dishes, feather beds, blankets, quilts, and cash. The report says that prairie fires burned through the area soon after the Indians left, and that many of the survivors went back East within ten days after the raid. The booklet also contains an article written for the Kansas Historical Society by the late William D. Street, who lived in Oberlin, who suggests that there was some connection between the massacre of Indians on the Sappa in 1875 and the massacre of settlers along the same creek and in the same area three years later.

Mari Sandoz, the author of *Cheyenne Autumn*, talked to many Cheyennes in doing research for her book, which is more about their long struggle with the Army and the Indian Agency than it is specifically about the Last Indian Raid. Mari Sandoz says that the Indians who took part in the raid were part of a band of 284 Cheyennes led by Chiefs Little Wolf and Dull Knife who had escaped from the reservation at Bent's Fort, in Indian Territory (Oklahoma), and were heading north across the state of Kansas, trying to get back to their old homeland in the Yellowstone country or rejoin their allies the Sioux at the Red Cloud Indian Agency, in northwestern Nebraska. She says that most of the band were Northern Cheyennes who had been sent to the reservation of the Southern Cheyennes in 1877. She says that the Northern Cheyennes caught malaria and starved in the south but that the Indian Agent and the Army would not let them leave, so on a night in early September 1878, they sneaked away from their camp, leaving their fires burning, and headed north—men, women, old people, and children. She says that they escaped many times from the cavalry that was sent after them, and they held off the cavalry in several engagements, and they raided in northwestern Kansas, and they crossed into Nebraska, where they camped on the banks of the Republican River, and then they split into two groups, and one group was captured and taken to Fort Robinson, in Nebraska, and when they found they were to be sent south again they escaped from the fort and were again captured and many of them were killed, and several of the men were taken back to Kansas to stand trial for murder but were acquitted for lack of evidence, and finally they and the others who remained of the Fort Robinson group were allowed to go to the Red

Cloud Agency, where they had wanted to go in the first place, while the second group avoided capture longer, and then the Army caught up with them, and finally they, too, were allowed to stay in the north, on land that is now the Northern Cheyenne Indian Reservation, in southeastern Montana. She says that about a third of the original band did not survive the trip. She says that some of the band were Southern Cheyennes, who came at least part of the way, and that it was probably the Southern Cheyennes who were mostly responsible for the killings in Kansas, since the Indians who had been attacked along the banks of the Sappa three years before were Southern Cheyennes and not Northern Cheyennes. She says that one member of the original band was an artist named Little Finger Nail, who recorded his and his tribe's exploits in colored pencil in a canvas-bound ledger book, and that he wore this book on his body and it was pierced by two .45-70 rifle bullets when he was killed after the escape from Fort Robinson, and that the book is now on display at the American Museum of Natural History. She says that some members of the band were men named Hog, Left Hand, Tangle Hair, Noisy Walker, Woodenthigh, Thin Elk, Black Coyote, Porcupine, and Black Crane and women named Short Woman, Comes in Sight, Singing Cloud, Pawnee Woman, and Buffalo Calf Road. She says that although the Cheyennes lost many women and children when they were attacked on Sand Creek in Colorado

in 1864, on the Washita in 1868, and on the Sappa
Creek in 1875, the Cheyennes themselves never killed
women or children.

The Indians were supposed to arrive Friday evening
of the centennial weekend. On Friday afternoon,
Esther Kump, Mrs. Claar's assistant, got a telephone
call from someone at the Northern Cheyenne Reservation, in Busby, Montana, saying that the Indians'
bus had broken down and they would not be able to
make it.

All weekend long, the loud screen door of the museum banged, the floor creaked, children's feet scuffed,
the phone rang, the air-conditioner turned off and on,
mothers told children to behave, and women in pioneer bonnets and hoopskirts talked to each other at
the butter-churning, china-painting, quiltmaking, and
other booths. On the street, venders sold vases, lamps,
bookends, lawn sprinklers, and clothes. Saturday
afternoon, a high-pitched, bratty engine noise could
be heard all over town as the toy tractors tried to pull
a toy trailer loaded with lead weights the length of a
sixteen-foot wooden table in the mini-tractor pull.
That evening, the senior citizens' group from Topeka
put on their medicine show, a collection of songs,
skits, and jokes (Sample joke: Man: "Little girl, is

your mother at home?" Girl: "Oh, she's 'round in the rear." Man: "I know *that*. I asked you is she at home!"), in the museum's large metal prefab auxiliary building, and the stage was set up in such a way that latecomers in the audience had to enter across the stage, through the same entrance that the actors used. The people who were sitting and watching edited from the action onstage the occasional passage of relatives, friends, or neighbors as easily as the eye edits ghosts from a television picture. On Saturday night there was a street dance, with the museum's four-piece band and a square-dance caller performing on top of a truck, and a group of ten semi-professional square dancers. The dance was held on South Penn Avenue, right before the avenue crosses the railroad tracks and becomes a dirt road, under mercury street lamps, which threw light of silvery green and electric blue on the dancers and the bystanders and the steep-shadowed grain elevators in the background. The street was as wide as a New York City avenue, made of reddish bricks, and slightly canted. While I was watching, only the ten semi-professional dancers danced, and on the street's breadth, under the harsh mercury light, their weaving, unweaving, crossing, recrossing, exchanging, promenading, short-petticoat rustling, and boot-heel clicking seemed like an inexplicable organic structure on a microscope slide. Around the part of the street set aside for dancing, cars pulled up, facing toward the center with their lights on, and under the square-dance music you could hear the many different-sounding engines idling in unison.

The biggest event of the centennial weekend was the tour of the sites of the Last Indian Raid, sponsored by the High Plains Preservation of History Commission. It was on Sunday. The sky was CinemaScope blue, and the weather was so dry you could strike a match on the inside of your nose. After a short memorial service at the Oberlin Cemetery, people got into their cars and formed a long column heading for the first of ten stops on the tour. The sixty-seven cars, vans, pickup trucks, motor homes, and Land-Rovers quickly left the asphalt highway for dirt roads, following the tour leaders, Mr. and Mrs. Fred Wallsmith (ranchers and amateur historians from Levant, Kansas), and the dust became so thick that sometimes you could see nothing of the car ahead except a small piece of light on the chrome of the rear-window molding. At other times, the wind came up, and you could see the vehicles ahead, all with tails of dust exactly the same size and blown in the same shape. When the head of the column turned off to the right or the left, people in the cars at the back of the column could see the dust of the head cars miles across the prairie. Most of the stops on the tour were along the Beaver and Sappa Creeks—spring-fed creeks that used to have water in even the most severe droughts but now are sometimes completely dry, because deep-drilling for irrigation has lowered the water table. The cotton-wood trees along the creeks were a dusty green, and some of the aspens had already turned yellow. Big, testy pheasants looked at the caravan from the burnt buffalo grass.

Two hundred and fourteen people signed a register on a clipboard that was passed around at the early stops; some of them signed "Mr. and Mrs. and Family," so there must have been more than that. Many of the people on the tour were blond and blue-eyed and tanned. Many of the children were so blond their hair was almost white. There was one Spanish-speaking family, who never got out of their car but seemed to be having a fine time. There were three graduate students with long hair; when they got out of their car, they locked it. At each stop, the children would play, and the teenagers would sit on the hoods of the cars and lean against the cars, and the parents and old people would stand holding babies and listen as Fred Wallsmith read from his paper about the Indian raid into a battery-powered loudspeaker and pointed out where the Indians rode from and where the settlers were killed a hundred years ago.

At one of the stops, Mrs. Keith Hall (maiden name Fern Anthony), a daughter of an eyewitness of the raid, made a speech on a hill overlooking the place where her family's farmhouse used to be:

"My grandfather was a contractor and builder in Bucks County, Pennsylvania, and he hurt himself—he fell through a building and broke his ribs. So in 1873

Grandfather and Grandmother and their children came West in a covered wagon, and that was when my father, Henry Anthony, was born, in California, Missouri, on Christmas Day, 1873. They came to Decatur County in February of 1874 and started a home three miles south of Oberlin, but then a man named Ireland came along and said that the land they were on was his. The neighbors said Ireland hadn't ever done anything with it, but Grandfather said no, there was plenty of land for everybody, so they moved nine miles up the Sappa from Oberlin and built a dugout from native limestone.

"In April of 1876, Grandfather had gone for supplies to Buffalo Station, which was the largest town near here with the supplies that one would need, and he got caught in a snowstorm. It became real bad real fast and Grandfather became snow-blind, so he let the horses have their heads and he tied the lines around the wagon brake and the horses found their way to the Kaus place. Grandfather had blisters on his eyeballs, so Mrs. Kaus scraped seed potatoes and put the raw scrapings on his eyes, and after a few days he could see well enough to get home. But he was never well after that, and he died in February of 1877, leaving Grandmother, who was twenty-eight years of age, nine miles from Oberlin, with five young children.

"In September of 1878, there was a rumor of Indians. Papa's oldest brother, Harry, was thirteen, and he ran to the house about nine o'clock one morning and said that he had seen some Indians shoot our neighbors, Mr. Smith and Mr. Hudson. A man named Lynch who was running his cattle in the area and a sixteen-year-old boy who was helping him were at our place that morning, and Grandmother was making breakfast for them. They went and called the children to the house.

"Papa was four years old. He would be five years old that Christmas. He came running to the house, but then he stopped on the hillside above the house—the dugout was built down in the hillside—and he sat down and started picking the cactus out of his feet. And he saw Mr. Laing and his son William going down the creek road that ran in front of our place in their wagon, taking the Van Cleve girls, Mary and Eliza, to school. He saw the Indians ride up to them, shake hands with them, and shoot them. The Indians cut the harnesses off the horses and took the horses, and they took the Van Cleve girls, too, but then they let the girls go.

"Papa's sister, Belle, ran up and picked him up and took him in the house, and the Indians came to the house and tried to get in and Mr. Lynch killed one of them when the Indian stuck his head in the window. Then the Indians went on up the Sappa and they did the same thing to the other people they found. They'd ride up to them, shake hands with them, and shoot them, and then cut the harnesses off the horses.

"Later on in the day, Mrs. Laing came to our place from their farm, about three miles up the creek. She said, 'I suppose my husband and son are killed,' and

Grandmother said yes. That evening, eight bodies in all were taken from the North Sappa back to Oberlin, and coffins were built for them, and they were buried by their friends and family.

"The soldiers who were supposed to stop the Indians were always behind, and the settlers thought that the soldiers sympathized with the Indians. But really the Indians were not to be blamed for a lot of the things that they did. After all, this was their land. I know we would fight if someone came and tried to take our land.

"Papa grew up and stayed there on the farm, and he built a house on top of the old dugout, and that's where he brought his bride—my mother, Alice Gilmore. And that is where I was born, eighty years ago this April 5."

Mrs. Hall received the only loud and spontaneous applause of the whole tour. Later, she said to me, "You know, I'm just as glad the Indians couldn't come."

After the tour, Mr. and Mrs. Wallsmith took the three graduate students and me to see Cheyenne Hole, where the Cheyennes were killed in 1875. The graduate students had looked for it once before but hadn't been able to find it, but Mr. Wallsmith knew where it was, because in 1975 he was at a memorial service that the High Plains Preservation of History Commission held at the site. Cheyenne Hole is on the

Middle Sappa Creek, about thirteen miles south of
the town of Atwood, Kansas, on land now owned by
a wheat-and-cattle farmer named Larry Curtin. We
stopped at his farmhouse, and he and his wife and his
children and his dog came out and got into a pickup
truck, and we followed them for a short distance and
stopped on a ridge. The sites where the settlers were
killed, which we had visited earlier in the day, had all
seemed like random X's on the prairie, but Cheyenne
Hole was different. Cheyenne Hole was a ruin. Lack-
ing crumbling temples and broken obelisks, it still
had a strong spirit of place-time in residence, the way
all ruins do. It was once, and for a long time, as real a
place to Indians as Peachtree Center, in Atlanta, is to
us. For centuries up to 1875, it was a great campsite.
The creek, which did not use to be dry, makes a wide
oxbow between two ridges. There are plenty of trees
and cover. The land along the creek is level, and the
ridges on either side protect it against the Great Plains
wind.

"My daddy owned this land before me," said Larry
Curtin, "and when I was little it wasn't nothin' to find
an arrowhead or a piece of pottery or some beads.
They were just lying all over the ground. After the
1875 massacre, I'm told, they buried twenty-seven
Indians right over there, about halfway between here
and the creek bed, under that soapweed. They buried
the chief in a cave up there." He pointed to the ridge
opposite. "See—even with that silo."

The sun had just set. Fred and Wilma Wallsmith,

Larry Curtin's wife, the graduate students, and I all kind of bunched together and sighted along Larry Curtin's arm to see where he was pointing, and then he turned away and started talking and joking with Fred Wallsmith. The rest of us were still peering in the direction of the cave when a falling star dropped perpendicular to the horizon right where we were looking, like a heavenly visual aid. The star started out white and turned pale green as it entered the lighter sky near the horizon. It was really an amazing thing to happen, but Fred Wallsmith and Larry Curtin did not see it, and the rest of us did not know each other well enough to comment on it.

An Angler at Heart

❖

Often during the past seven years, I have taken a walk from the offices of *The New Yorker* along Forty-third Street—across Fifth Avenue, across Madison Avenue, across Vanderbilt Avenue—then through Grand Central Terminal, across Lexington Avenue, up to Forty-fourth Street, into the elevator at 141 East Forty-fourth Street, up to the third floor, and through the belled door of a small fishing-tackle shop called the Angler's Roost, whose sole proprietor is a man named Jim Deren. Since I've been taking this walk, the Biltmore Men's Bar, which I used to pass at the corner of Madison and Forty-third, changed to the Biltmore Bar, which then became a different bar, named the Café Fanny, which was replaced by a computer store called Digital's, which moved (along with

a lot of other stores on the block) after the Biltmore
Hotel closed and disappeared under renovators' scaf-
folding. Once, on this walk, I had to detour around
some barricades inside Grand Central, because a film
crew was working on the movie *Superman*. Valerie
Perrine and Gene Hackman were supposedly there,
but I did not see them. Since then, I have seen the
movie in a theater, and have noted the part that the
crew must have been working on when I passed by.
During these seven years, the huge Kodak display in
the station near the Lexington Avenue wall, which
people say ruins the station's interior light and makes
it difficult to distinguish the beautiful Venetian-
summer-night starscape on the ceiling, has featured
photographs of water-skiers behind motorboats, a
Bicentennial celebration with men dressed as Continental soldiers, the Pyramid of the Sun at Teotihua-
cán (by night, lighted), the opening ceremonies of the
Winter Olympics at Lake Placid, the Great Wall of
China, and, one spring, a closeup shot of a robin,
which looked frightening at that size. One time, I
came in through the door at Forty-third Street and
there before me, across the echoing well of the con-
course, was a view of a rock-cluttered desert, barn-red
under a pink sky, with a little piece of the foot of a
space probe visible in the foreground—Mars, photo-
graphed by Viking 2.

A fisherman can look at some sections of any trout
stream clean enough for fish to live in, and say with

confidence, A large fish lives there. The water should be deep, and it should be well aerated; that is, it should be free-flowing, rich in oxygen, and not stagnant. There should be a source of food: a grassy bank with beetles, grasshoppers, field mice, and frogs; or a little tributary creek with minnows, chubs, dace, and sculpins; or an upstream section with a silt bottom for large, burrowing mayfly nymphs. There should be cover—downed logs, overhanging tree branches, undercut banks. Where these conditions are found, the chances are very good that at least one large fish will be found as well. Such sections of a river are called good lies. A good lie will usually have a good fish lying in wait, gently finning, looking upstream for whatever the current may bring him.

I have always thought that, as lies go, it would be hard to find a better one than Grand Central Terminal. It is deep—water that deep would be a dark blue. Aerated streams of humanity cascade down the escalators from the Pan Am Building, and flow from the rest of midtown, the rest of the city, the rest of the world, through trains and subways and airport buses and taxis, into its deep pool and out again, and the volume of this flow makes it rich in the important nutrient called capital. Well, in this good lie the big fish of the fishing-tackle business is Jim Deren, of the Angler's Roost. For over forty years, he has had a shop in the area—a shop that has outlasted changes in fishing fashions, changes in the economy, competitors who gave their shops names intentionally similar to his, and finally even Abercrombie & Fitch, his biggest local competitor, which closed in 1977. All this time, Deren has remained in his good lie, gently finning behind the counter in his shop, consulting with fishermen from just about every place where there's water, selling every kind of angling supply imaginable, taking in cash and checks as gracefully as a big brown trout sips mayflies from the surface of a Catskill stream.

The first time I met Jim Deren, I was looking for a particular dry fly (a pattern called the Gold-Ribbed Hare's Ear, with a body that goes all the way back over the bend of the hook), which had worked well for me in Wyoming, and which I could not find anywhere. I came across the entry for the Angler's Roost in the Yellow Pages:

ANGLER'S ROOST
FISHING TECHNICIANS
Tackle, Salt & Fresh, Lures, Flies
Fly Materials, Waders & Clothing
Repairs, Books & Advertising Props
JIM DEREN ADVISOR

That impressed me. I called the shop one Saturday afternoon around six o'clock, and was surprised to find Deren there. In later years, I have learned that he is in his shop at all hours: I have found him in at seven-fifteen on a beautiful Sunday evening in June; I have found him in on all sorts of holidays, when midtown is nothing but blowing papers. On that first Saturday, Deren told me that he was about to go home but that if I came in soon he would wait for me. I arrived at the shop half an hour later. He did not happen to have the exact fly I wanted, but he told me where to get it. We talked for a while, and I left without buying anything—the only time that has ever happened.

A few months later, during a really warm April, I decided I had to go fishing, even though I had never been fishing in the East and knew nothing about it. I bought a fishing license at the Department of Environmental Conservation office on the sixty-first floor of the World Trade Center, and then I went to see Deren. He told me the book to buy—*New Streamside Guide to Naturals and Their Imitations,* by Art Flick. He said that, because it had been so warm, certain mayflies that would usually be on the stream later in the season might have already appeared. He sold me flies imitating those insects. He told me where to fish —in the Beaverkill, the Little Beaverkill, and Willowemoc Creek, near Roscoe, New York. He told me what bus to take. I left his shop, went back to my apartment, got my fly rod and sleeping bag, went to the Port Authority Bus Terminal, boarded a Short Line bus, and rode for two and a half hours with Hassidic Jews going to Catskill resorts and women going to upstate ashrams. On the bus, I read the *Streamside Guide,* which says that mayflies live for several years underwater as swimming nymphs, hatch into winged insects, mate while hovering over the water, lay their eggs in the water, and die; that recently hatched mayflies, called duns, float along the surface and are easy for trout to catch, and so are the stage of the mayfly's life cycle most sensible for the angler to imitate with artificials; that different species of mayflies hatch at different times of the year, according to water temperature; and that the different species emerge every year in an order so invariable as to be the only completely predictable aspect of trout fishing. I got off the bus in Roscoe about four in the afternoon, walked to the Beaverkill, hid my sleeping bag in some willows, set up my fly rod, and walked up the river until I reached a spot with no fishermen. I noticed mayflies in the air, noticed dragonflies zipping back and forth eating the mayflies. I saw a dragonfly pick a mayfly out of the air so neatly that he took only the body, leaving the two wings to flutter down to the surface of the stream and float away. I caught a mayfly myself after a lot of effort, compared it with the pictures in my *Streamside Guide,* decided that it was the male of the *Ephemerella subvaria* (Deren had been right; according to the book, that insect wasn't due for about two weeks more), tied on its imitation (a pattern called the Red Quill, in size 14), made a short cast, caught a little trout, made a few more short casts, caught another little trout, and waited while a fat guy with a spinning rod who said he wasn't having much luck walked by me up the river. Then I made a good, long cast under a spruce bough to a patch of deep water ringed with lanes of current, like a piece of land in the middle of a circular freeway-access ramp. This patch of water had a smooth, tense surface marked with little tucks where eddying water was boiling up from underneath. My fly sat motionless on this water for a time that when I replay it in my mind seems really long. Then a fish struck so hard it was like a person punching up through the water with his fist. Water splashed several feet in the air, and there was a flash of fish belly of that particular shade of white— like the white of a horse's eye when it's scared, or the white of the underside of poplar leaves blown by wind right before a storm—that often seems to accompany violence in nature. The fish ran downstream like crazy (I don't remember setting the hook), then he ran upstream, then he ran downstream again. He jumped several times—not arched and poised, as in the sporting pictures, but flapping back and forth so fast he was a blur. Line was rattling in my line guides; I was pulling it in and he was taking it out, until finally there was a big pile of line at my feet, and the fish, also, in the shallow water at my feet. He was a thirteen-inch brook trout, with a wild eye that was a circle of black set in a circle of gold. The speckles on his back reproduced the wormlike marks on the rocks on the stream bottom, and his sides were filled with colors—orange, red, silver, purple, midnight blue— and yet were the opposite of gaudy. I hardly touched him; he was lightly hooked. I released him, and after a short while he swam away. I stood for maybe ten minutes, with my fly rod lying on the gray, softball-size rocks, and I stared at the trees on the other side of the river. The feeling was like having hundreds of gag hand-buzzers applied to my entire body.

Since that day I have always loved the Red Quill dry fly, and particularly the Red Quill that Deren sells, which is the most elegant I have ever seen. For me, the Red Quill is a shamanistic medicine bundle that called forth the strike, the flash of belly, the living palette of colors from that spring day, and, years later, even in situations where it is not remotely the right fly, I find myself tying it on just to see what will happen.

Also since that day I have believed that Jim Deren is a great man. He is the greatest man I know of who will talk to just anybody off the street.

In appearance, Deren is piscine. He is stocky—prob-ably about five feet ten inches tall. His hair is in a mouse-brown brush cut, about half an inch long. His forehead is corrugated with several distinct wrinkles, which run up and down, like marks of soil erosion on a hill. His eyes are weak and watery and blue, behind thick glasses with thick black frames. There is a large amount of what looks like electrical tape around the glasses at the bridge. His eyebrows are cinnamon-colored. His nose is thick, and his lips are thick. He has a white mustache. His direct, point-blank regard can be unsettling. People who have fished their whole lives sometimes find themselves saying when they encounter this gaze that they don't know a thing about fishing, really. Deren has a style of garment which he loves and which he wears almost every single day in his shop. This garment is the jumpsuit. For a long time, he wore either a charcoal-gray jump-suit or an olive-green jumpsuit. One or both of the jumpsuits had a big ring on the zipper at the throat. Recently, Deren has introduced another jumpsuit into the repertoire. This is a sky-blue jumpsuit with a green-on-white emblem of a leaping bass on the left breast pocket. Deren's voice is deep and gravelly. I can do a good imitation of him. The only sentence I can think of that might make his accent audible on paper (in the last word, anyway) is one I have heard him speak several times while he was talking on one of his unfavorite topics, the "flower children": "In late October, early November, when we're driving back from fishing out West, with the wind howling and huge dark snow clouds behind us, sometimes we pass these frail girls, these flower children, standing by the side of the road in *shawwwwwwwwls*."

I say Deren is probably about five feet ten inches

tall because even though he often says, "I've been running around all day. I'm exhausted," I have actually seen him standing up only a few times. Like a psychiatrist, Deren is usually seated. I have seen him outside his shop only once—when, as I was leaving, he came down in the elevator to pick up a delivery on the first floor. (Ambulant, he seemed to me surprisingly nimble.) It is appropriate for Deren to be seated all the time, because he has tremendous repose. There is a lot of bad repose going around these days: the repose of someone watching a special Thursday-night edition of Monday Night Football; the repose of someone smoking a cigarette on a ten-minute break at work; the repose of driving; the repose of waiting in line at the bank. Deren is in his sixties. The fish he has caught, the troubles he has been through, the fishing tackle he has sold, the adventures he has had lend texture to his repose. On good days, his repose hums like a gyroscope.

Deren talking about the Angler's Roost while sitting in his shop on a slow afternoon in March: "It seems only natural that I would have gravitated to this business. I've been tying flies ever since I was in short pants. When I was in grade school in New Jersey, I used to go without lunch because I wanted to save my money and buy fishing tackle. I remember fashioning a fly from a jacket of mine when I was a kid just barely big enough to be let out of sight. I tied it out of a lumberjacket that my mother had made for me—"

The phone rings.

"Hello. Angler's Roost."

". . . . ."

"Christ, I don't know a thing about Chinese trout fishing, Doc."

". . . . ."

"Well, they gotta have trout fishing. The Japanese have trout fishing. Just the other day, I sold some stuff to Yasuo Yoshida, the Japanese zipper magnate. He's probably got more tackle than I got. He's *kichi* about trout fishing. *Kichi*—that's Japanese for nuts."

". . . . ."

"Well, I think the Russians should open one or two of their rivers for salmon fishing, certainly. They just have to have terrific salmon fishing."

". . . . ."

"Look at it this way—next time you'll know."

". . . . ."

"Whatever you find out, Doc, let me know when you get back. Have a good time.

"Anyway, I had this blue-gray lumberjacket, and there was this little blue fly on the water. The goddam fish weren't considering anything but this fly. Well, between the lining and the thread of my jacket, I made a fly that looked something like the insect, and so, glory be, after some effort I caught a fish. The fish made a mistake, and that did it. This was on a little stream in Pennsylvania, a little tributary of the Lehigh. It was a day as miserable as this, but later in the year."

Deren picks up a package of Keebler Iced Oatmeal and Raisin Cookies, breaks it open in the middle, and dumps all the contents into a white plastic quart bucket—the kind of bucket that ice cream comes in. He starts to eat the cookies.

"After that, I was really hooked. I collected all kinds of items for flytying. Cigarette and cigar wrappers, hairs from dogs. Christ, I cut hair off every goddam thing that was around. Picked up feathers in pet shops. I was always raiding chickens or ducks. I remember I tried to get some feathers from some geese and they ran me the hell out the county. Horse tails. Anything. It wasn't long before I was selling some of the flies I tied. As far as I know, I was the first commercial nymph-tier in the country. I was selling flies in New York, New Jersey, and fairly deep into Pennsylvania. Fishing was a great thing for me, now that I look back on it, because in a lot of the contact sports I was always busting my glasses. But row a boat—I had a pair of chest muscles, looked like a goddam weight lifter. I was very well coordinated. I had coordination and timing. That has something to do with fishing. I was a good wing shot."

Deren reaches under the counter and produces a banana. With a table knife, he cuts the banana in half. He eats one half, and leaves the other half, in the skin, on top of a pile of papers. Later, a customer will find in the pile of papers a copy of a fishing magazine that he has been looking for. He will take it out from under the half banana and buy it.

"I spent all my time in high school fishing, and one day I noticed this guy was watching me. He'd been watching me a few times before. He'd ask me questions. Well, it turned out this guy had a radio show about fishing and hunting. I think he called himself Bill the Fisherman. He started telling people about me—called me the Child Fisherman Prodigy. He told the proprietor of a fishing-tackle shop in the heart of Newark, right by Penn Station, and the man hired me, and eventually I became the youngest fishing-tackle buyer in the country. Not long after that, I was imported by an outfit in New York called Alex Taylor & Company, on Forty-second Street. I put them in the fishing-tackle business—"

The phone rings again.

"Angler's Roost."

". . . . . "

"We've got all kinds of hook hones."

". . . . . "

"Fresh and salt, both."

". . . . . "

"Yes, some of them are grooved."

". . . . . "

"Two different grooves."

". . . . . "

"Each one comes in a plastic case."

". . . . ."

"Different lengths. I think two-inch and three-inch."

". . . . ."

"What the hell do you mean, who makes it? It's a goddam hook hone! What the hell difference does it make who makes it?

"Guy wants to know who makes the hook hone. Wants to know what *brand* it is. Christ. Anyway, after that I became a buyer and salesman for another house, called Kirtland Brothers, downtown. They're now extinct. I advised their clients on the technical aspects of fly-fishing. Mainly, I handled their flytying material. About this time, I began my mail-order business, selling flytying material through ads in different magazines. I was working all day for Kirtland Brothers, then staying up all night to handle my mail orders. Finally, it got unmanageable as a side business. I wasn't doing justice to either job. I finished my obligations to that firm, and then I opened up the first Angler's Roost, at 207 East Forty-third, above where the Assembly Restaurant used to be. I dreamed up the name myself. You had the roost connotation because it was up off the street and you had guys that hung around all day with the eternal bull sessions. (I was thinking of selling coffee and cake there for a while.) Then you think of birds roosting, and, of course, a lot of what we sold was feathers. And a lot of the feathers were rooster feathers—capes and necks."

Deren takes from the pocket of his jumpsuit a new pack of True Blue cigarettes. With a flytying bodkin, he makes a number of holes all the way through the pack. Then he takes out a cigarette and lights it.

"Since its inception, the Roost has been tops in its field. We've had every kind of customer, from the bloated bondholder to the lowliest form of human life. Frank Jay Gould, the son of the railroad magnate, once bought a boat over my telephone. Ted Williams used to stop by whenever the Red Sox were in town. He was a saltwater fisherman, but we infected him with the salmon bug. We've had boxers, bandleaders, diplomats, ambassadors. Benny Goodman used to come in all the time. I sold Artie Shaw his salmon outfit. So many notable people, I don't even remember. Engelhard, of Engelhard precious metals. Marilyn Monroe's photographer, Milton Greene. Señor Wences—the ventriloquist who did the thing with the box. Bing Crosby. Tex Ritter. He was an uncle of mine by my first marriage; I got a lot of other customers in Nashville through him. We've had more than one President. Eisenhower came in once. He was a nice guy—didn't have his nose too far up in the air. We've had three generations of people come in here, maybe four. We've had some of the very elite. A lot of them don't want their names mentioned."

Deren looks left, cocks his wrist as if he were throwing a dart, and flips the cigarette out of sight behind the counter.

"We had our own television show, which ran for twenty-six weeks on the old DuMont Television Network. It was called The Sportsman's Guide. It was sponsored by Uhu Glue—a miracle glue, kind of like Krazy Glue. The announcer was a guy named Connie Evans. I did the lecturing—like on a spinning reel— and then when we did a fishing trip I did the fishing. That television show wasn't on very long before people started calling me Uncle Jimmy. I don't know how it got started, but it stuck. I was also a technical panelist on a radio show called The Rod and Gun Club of the Air. The other panelists and I shot the breeze amongst us every week."

A blond woman in a beige knit ski cap comes in. She asks Deren if he has an eight-foot bamboo fly rod. He says he doesn't but he can order one for her. The woman says, "Oh, that's great. I think he might marry me if I find him that rod." She leaves.

"Did I tell you about our television show? The Sportsman's Guide? Did I tell you about our heavy involvement in the advertising field? Over the years, we've acted as consultant on hundreds and hundreds of ads. Sooner or later, everybody uses a fishing ad. Also, the slogan 'How's your love life?' started in the Roost. I used to ask my customers that when they came in, and then it became the slogan for a brand of toothpaste.

"We developed the first satisfactory big-game reel— the Penn 12/0 Senator. I guess there's six or seven miles of those things now. We also helped develop the

concept of R. and R.—Rest and Recuperation—for
the military. The idea was to take these guys who'd
been through the horrors of war, get them fishing, get
them flytying, get their minds off their former
troubles. Some of the stuff I wrote on flytying for the
Navy was posted in battleships that are now in moth-
balls. We also supplied the cord that made Dracula's
wings move, for the Broadway show. We've always
been an international business. Anglers come from
India, Australia, New Zealand, Tasmania, Norway,
Iceland, Ireland, Holland, Germany, France, Italy,
Switzerland, Canada, Mexico, South Africa, South
America—so many South Americans you'd think it
was just next door, and they're all loaded. Bolivia,
Tierra del Fuego. Any guy who's a nut about a fly
comes to the Roost eventually. Anyplace a trout swims,
they know the Roost. Not only trout. Also bonefish,
tarpon, sailfish, striped bass, salmon—"

The phone rings again.

"Angler's Roost."

". . . . ."

"Hello, my little pigeon."

". . . . ."

"Just a few minutes. I'm leaving right now."

In Deren's shop, three customers can stand comfort-
ably. You can stand and put your hands in your
pockets, but there really isn't room to move around
much. Four is tight. Five is crowded. Six is very

crowded. When there are six customers in the shop, one of them has to hold on to somebody to keep from falling over backward into the knee-high wader bin. Except for the small space around the customers' feet, Deren's shop is 360 degrees of fishing equipment, camping equipment, books, and uncategorizable stuff. The shop is like a forest in that if you remain silent in either of them for any length of time you will hear something drop.

"What the hell was that?"

"I think it was a book."

"Don't worry about it. Leave it there."

"*Better Badminton?* Jim, how come you have a book called *Better Badminton?*"

"A lot of these things get shipped by mistake, and then it's too goddam much trouble to send them back."

In Deren's shop, he has tackle for the three different kinds of sportfishing—bait casting, spin fishing, and fly-fishing. Bait-casting outfits are the standard rod and reel that cartoonists usually give to fishermen. The reel has a movable spool, and both rod and reel are designed for bait or for lures heavy enough to be cast with their own weight. Spin-fishing rods and reels are also designed for lures heavy enough to be cast with their own weight, but because of refinements in the reel—a non-movable spool that allows the line to spiral off—spin-fishing rods cast farther with less weight. In fly-fishing, the lure is usually nothing but feathers on a hook, so it does not have enough weight to be cast. Fly-fishing equipment consists of longer, lighter rods and a thick, tapered line, which work together with a whipping action to cast the fly. All three of these kinds of fishing can be done in either fresh or salt water. The sea is bigger than the land; saltwater tackle is usually bigger and heavier than freshwater tackle. Deren sells saltwater rods as thick as mop handles, and freshwater fly rods like Seiji Ozawa's baton. They are made of bamboo, fiberglass, metal, or (recent developments) graphite or boron. He sells reels like boat winches, and palm-size reels that sound like Swiss watches when you crank them. He has thousands of miles of line—nylon monofilament or braided nylon or plastic or braided Dacron or silk or wire. He has hooks from size 28, which are small enough to fit about five on a fingertip, to size 16/o, which have a four-inch gap between the point of the hook and the shank.

Deren also has:

thousands of lures designed to imitate live game-fish prey, with names like Bass-Oreno, Original Spin-Oreno, Buzz'n Cobra, Chugger, Lucky 13, Crazy Crawler, Hopkins No-Eql, Goo-Goo Eyes, Hula Popper, Jitterbug, Devil's Horse, Creek Chub Wiggle Fish, Flatfish, Lazy Ike, Red Eye, Dardevle, Fluke Slayer, Ava Diamond Jig, Rapala, Dancing Doll Jig, Rebel, Darter, Mirrolure, Shyster, Abu-Reflex, Swedish Wobbler, Hawaiian Wiggler, Golden-Eye Troublemaker, Hustler, Al's Goldfish, Pikie Minnow, Salty Shrimper, Williams Wobbler, Tiny Tad, Tiny Torpedo, Zara (named after Zarragossa Street, the former red-light district in Pensacola, Florida, because of its attractive wiggle);

countless trout flies that imitate mayflies at every stage of their life, with names like Quill Gordon, Hendrickson, March Brown, Red Quill, Grey Fox, Lady Beaverkill, Light Cahill, Grey Fox Variant, Dun Variant, Cream Variant, Blue-Winged Olive, Sulphur Dun, Brown Drake, Green Drake, Pale Evening Dun, Little White-Winged Black;

trout flies that imitate other insects—the Letort Hopper, Jassid, Black Ant, Red Ant, Cinnamon Ant, Black Gnat, Spider, Leaf Roller, Stonefly, Caddis, Case Caddis, Caddis Worm, Caddis Pupa, Dragonfly, Hellgrammite, Damselfly;

flies that imitate mice, frogs, and bats;

streamer flies—the Muddler Minnow, Spruce Fly, Spuddler, Professor, Supervisor, Black Ghost, Grey Ghost, Mickey Finn—which are probably meant to imitate minnows;

other flies—the Parmachenee Belle, Lord Baltimore, Yellow Sally, Adams, Rat-Faced McDougal, Woolly Worm, Hare's Ear, Humpy, Royal Coachman, Hair-Wing Royal Coachman, Lead-Wing Coachman, Queen of the Waters, Black Prince, Red Ibis—of which it is hard to say just what they are supposed to imitate, and which are sometimes called attractor flies;

big, colorful salmon flies, with names like Nepisi-
quit, Abbey, Thunder and Lightning, Amherst, Black
Fairy, Orange Blossom, Silver Doctor, Dusty Miller,
Hairy Mary, Lancelot, Jock Scott, Fair Duke, Durham
Ranger, Marlodge, Fiery Brown, Night Hawk, Black
Dose, Warden's Worry;

flies that he invented himself—Deren's Stonefly,
Deren's Fox, Deren's Harlequin, The Fifty Degrees,
The Torpedo, The Black Beauty, Deren's Speckled
Caddis, Deren's Cream Caddis, Deren's Cinnamon
Caddis, Deren's Grey Caddis;

feathers for tying flies—rooster (domestic and foreign, winter plumage and summer plumage, dozens of
shades), ostrich, goose, kingfisher, mallard, peacock,
turkey, imitation jungle cock, imitation marabou,
imitation wood duck;

fur—Alaskan seal, arctic fox, mink, beaver, weasel,
imitation chinchilla, raccoon, ermine, rabbit, fitch,
marten, gray fox, skunk, squirrel, civet cat—also for
tying flies;

hair—deer, bear, antelope, moose, goat, elk, badger,
calf—also for tying flies;

scissors, forceps, pliers, razors, vises, lamps, tweezers,
bobbins, bodkins, floss, thread, chenille, tinsel, Mylar,
lead wire, wax, yarn—also for tying flies;

chest waders, wader suspenders, wader belts, wader
cleats, wader racks, wader patch kits, wading shoes,
wading staffs, hip boots, boot dryers, inner boot soles,
Hijack brand V-notch boot removers, insulated socks,

fishing vests, bug-repellent fishing vests, rain pants, ponchos, head nets, long-billed caps, hunting jackets, thermal underwear, high-visibility gloves, fishing shirts;

ice augers, dried grasshoppers, minnow scoops, fish stringers, hook disgorgers, rubber casting weights, gigs, spears, car-top rod carriers, rubber insect legs, fish-tank aerators, English game bags, wicker creels, folding nets, hand gaffs, worm rigs, gasoline-motor starter cords, watercolor paintings of the Miramichi River, sponge-rubber bug bodies, line straighteners, knot-tiers, snakebite kits, hatbands, leather laces, salmon eggs, plastic-squid molds, stuff you spray on your glasses so they won't fog up, duck and crow calls, waterproof match cases, lead split-shot, collapsible oars, bells that you hook up to your line so they ring when a fish takes your bait, Justrite electric head lanterns, dried mayfly nymphs, rescue whistles, canteens, butterfly nets, peccary bristles, porcupine quills, frog harnesses . . .

The truth is, I have no idea of all the things Deren has in his shop. Just about every item he sells is appropriate to a particular angling situation. In addition to the part of the shop that the customer sees, the Angler's Roost fills a couple of large back rooms, a lot of space in an office on another floor of the same building, and space that Deren rents in a warehouse in New Jersey. I have not yet encountered, nor would I encounter in several lifetimes of angling, all the different situations for which the different items in his shop are intended.

Deren likes to recite certain fishing maxims over and over, and although he says his intent is purely educational ("We don't sell anybody. We advise, and then they do their own buying") I have seen his maxims work on customers' wallets the way oyster knives work on oysters. One of these maxims is "Ninety percent of a trout's diet consists of food he finds underwater." A customer who hears this often decides he has to have a couple dozen stone-fly nymphs—weighted flies that imitate the nymphal stage of the stone fly, an insect common in rocky streambeds. The stone fly that Deren sells is two dollars, which makes it one of the more expensive trout flies he sells. Another maxim is "Trout don't always see a floating mayfly from underneath; when a trout is taking a fly he will break the surface"—here Deren does an imitation of a trout regarding with bulging eye a fly at eye level—"and when he does he sees that the back of the insect is darkly vermiculated." A customer who hears this may conclude that he cannot be without several flies—in the pattern called Deren's Fox, as it happens—that have across the back a number of stripes made with a bodkin dipped in lacquer, to suggest the dark vermiculations. (Deren's imitation of a trout breaking the surface and seeing a fly is itself worth the price of a lot of Deren's Foxes.) Another maxim is "People always say that a fly reel is nothing more than a storage case for line, but this is not true. A fly reel has many functions it must perform. It has to be the right weight, it has to be the right size to hold the proper amount of line, and it has to have a smooth drag"—the mechanism that controls the amount of resistance offered to a fish pulling line off the reel—"which can be adjusted to the various situations you may encounter." Another maxim, one of Deren's most serviceable, which often comes up when a customer is contemplating an unusually expensive purchase, is "The money may not seem worth it, but when you run across a fish you've waited your whole life to catch and then lose him because your equipment was substandard—well, then the money becomes immaterial."

One spring, just before I was going to Key West to visit my grandmother, Deren got me in the pincers of the last two maxims as I was deciding on a new fly reel: people say a fly reel is just a storage case for line but you need a good reel with a good drag, etc.; and if you buy a substandard (i.e., cheaper) reel and because of it lose the fish of your life, etc. I was planning to wade the tidal flats around the islands fly-fishing for bonefish and permit (a kind of pompano), of which the first is supposed to be very difficult to catch and the second is supposed to be about impossible to catch. Like a lot of people before me and after me, I cracked. I spent $110 on an English-made reel with level adjustable drag, which came in a fleece-lined suede case. The first day, I fished with it at a fishing spot that had been recommended by a guy behind the counter at a bait-and-tackle shop called Boog Powell's Anglers Marine (it is owned by the former baseball star, but I have never seen him in there), on Stock Island, the key just up from Key West. This fishing spot was a long sandbar behind the Boca Chica Naval Air Station, the military installation that sometimes used to appear on TV as a piece of runway and an airplane wing and some heat shimmers in the background of news stories about Cuban refugees. My cousin dropped me off there. She had to take the car back to get the seats reupholstered. (My grandmother spends a lot of time driving people in wet bathing suits around, so her seat covers always fall apart.) I hid my lunch, which my grandmother had packed for me, in the mangroves. Black mangroves, since they grow in or near water, have hundreds of little breathing tubes that aerate their roots and look like Bic pen tops sticking up from the mud. As I waded out, I scared up a couple of shore birds, which made regularly spaced splashes with their feet on the surface of the water as they took off. The sandbar, a line of white between turquoise water and dark-blue water, was maybe a quarter mile out. I had to wade in up to my armpits at one point. I was nervous. I had never heard of a wading angler being eaten by a shark, but I didn't know why. It seemed as if anything that wanted to come in and get me could. At one point, I almost stepped on a ray, which stirred up big clouds of mud as it winged away. I was doubly scared when I realized that my fear was probably releasing chemicals into the water which would call predators in from all over the ocean. On the sandbar, the water was ankle-deep. I worked my way along, casting to the deep water on the ocean side of the bar. It was very windy, and I kept hitting myself between the shoulder blades with the weighted fly when I cast. I saw one fish over the half mile of sandbar that I covered. I'm not sure what kind of fish it was—I don't think it was a permit or a bonefish. It was about two feet long. It wasn't expecting to find anybody standing in the water out there. About ten feet from me, it saw me, and it did the closest thing to a double take I've ever seen a fish do. Then it disappeared like the Road Runner in the cartoon, with a ricochet noise. I waded back to shore, stepping on crunching white coral and then slogging through a long patch of grayish-white ooze—the kind of muck that dinosaurs left footprints in. I was quite a distance from where I'd left my lunch. I began to walk back along the road. As I came around a bend in the road, I saw a camper parked. It had Alabama license plates. About the same time I saw the camper, I heard the jingle of a dog collar. With one bark, a Great Dane plunged out of the bushes toward me. A second later, a dachshund and a border collie, both barking a lot, came out of the bushes. The Great Dane came up to my shoulder, and had a mouth—filled with yellow, pointed teeth—that could have eaten a clock radio. A man and a woman were sunbathing on deck chairs near the camper. The man did not get up. The woman told me to hold still and the dog wouldn't bite me. I held still, and the dog bit me in the right shoulder. I told the woman that the dog was biting me. The border collie was nipping around my knees, the dachshund around my ankles. The Great Dane bit me in the right buttock. The woman was putting on her sandals. The Great Dane bit me hard next to my left shoulder blade. The woman came up and pulled him off. I walked a distance away, and then I raised my shirt and turned my back to the woman and asked her if I was bleeding. She said I wasn't. I walked on up the road. The dachshund continued to nip around my ankles for a way up the road. The woman was calling him. His name was Fritz. I got to the place in the mangroves where I'd left my lunch, and I found my lunch and sat down on a mangrove root. My shirt was not torn where the dog had bitten me in the right shoulder, and my pants weren't torn where the dog had bitten me in the right buttock. But the lower back of my shirt was torn, with several long tooth holes. I felt my back. I had two puncture wounds, and they were bleeding. I walked back to where the camper had been parked, shouting for the people to hold the dog. The camper was not there anymore. (I later found out that the state of Florida requires that any time a dog bites a person it must be locked up for ten days to see if it has rabies. The Alabamians, possibly having had this kind of experience before, and not wanting to change their vacation plans, may have left the minute

I was out of sight.) I ate my lunch and thought about
what I should do. I decided that the dog probably did
not have rabies but was just crazy and overbred, like
many Great Danes. I decided that it would not be
worth it to try to get back to Key West—that it made
more sense to wait for my cousin to come and pick me
up. I wasn't going to bleed to death. I went back out
and fished some more, seeing this time not a single
fish. However, I did spot a yellow object floating by
me and snagged it with my rod, and the object turned
out to be a plastic toy man—part of the Fisher-Price
toy dump truck recommended for ages two to six. I
put it in my pocket, because at that time my cousin's
daughter really liked Fisher-Price toys. I kept hearing
voices shouting back and forth along the shore. When
my cousin finally blew the horn for me and I went in,
I learned that the voices had belonged, probably, to
whoever had been engaged in stringing coils of barbed
wire along the shoreline. (Probably it was the Seabees
putting out the wire for airfield security.) This barbed
wire had barbs on it shaped like little meat cleavers.
I made it through the first two coils, but I got tangled
up in the third coil, cutting my legs in several places.
When I got to the car and dismantled my fly rod, I
broke off a line guide. My cousin's daughter was with
her, and she was very happy with the Fisher-Price man
I'd found. My cousin took me to the de Poo Hospital,
in Key West, where a twenty-nine-year-old doctor
with long hair, from Chillicothe, Ohio, who had de-

cided to practice in Key West because he hated the winters in Ohio, told me that there hadn't been a case of rabies in Florida in a really long time and that house dogs like Great Danes almost never got rabies anyway, but that I should have a tetanus shot, so I did, and it cost thirty dollars. I didn't go out fishing, or even think about fishing, for a few days after this, with the result that I forgot to rinse the salt water out of the works of my expensive new reel, with the result that the works corroded to the point where the reel would turn approximately as much as the Chrysler Building turns on its foundation. Now the reel sits on my desk, proving Daren's maxim; more than a storage case for line, it is also a paperweight.

Although all kinds of people go to Deren's shop, most of his customers are adult white men. This category is large enough to include many subcategories. Some of these men are technicians; they wear raincoats, gray Glen-plaid suits, black-orange-and-yellow striped ties, and gray plaid Irish walking caps, and the gleam of their metal-rimmed glasses reinforces the expression of scientific curiosity in their eyes. They know no higher words of praise than "state of the art." When Deren shows them the latest graphite fly rod, they ask, "So is this pretty much state of the art in graphite rods?" Others are rich, and probably social. They bring with them the warm, Episcopal smell of Brooks

Brothers or the Union Club, and they talk like George Plimpton: "An *English*man who fishes in *Brazil* had this particular kind of *lanyard,* do you know the kind I mean, *marvelous,* yes, that's exactly what I want, yes, *good* for you!" Others are writers or photographers or painters; they are quiet or loud, hung over or not hung over, and many of them carry shoulder bags and don't wear suits and look as if somebody had smudged them when they were wet. Others are short, bluff, bald men who look like walking thumbs and laugh after every sentence they speak; sometimes they open the door and yell "Hey, mister! Got any hooks?" and then they laugh delightedly. Others are terse. That's what they do for a living. They're professionally terse: "Jim. Ask you a question. Winchester. Model 21. Twenty gauge." Others are executives in the oil business who are leaving tomorrow for Bahrain. Once, I heard the executives in the elevator going up to Deren's talking about the management characteristics of different oil companies. One of them said that top management at Mobil Oil suffered from "paralysis by analysis." Others are big, wear size-11 shoes, have red faces, and come into the shop in the afternoon with cocktails and good lunch on their breath, and shoot the bull with Deren for hours.

Guy: "Jimmy, let me ask you something and you tell me what you think of this. Last August, I was sitting on the bank of a river in Michigan waiting for it to cool off and for the fish to start feeding, and I saw this white thing bouncing along the river bottom, and when it got close enough I saw that it was a peeled potato, and when it came closer I saw that a twelve- or thirteen-inch trout was *bouncing* the potato along the river bottom with his nose—"

Deren: "You sure it was a potato?"

Guy: "It was either a peeled potato or maybe a peeled apple. This trout was bouncing it; I swear, he was dribbling it with his nose along the bottom like a ball. Friend of mine and I followed him downstream a long way. He just kept dribbling that potato. Now, what in the hell could that have been?"

Deren: "I don't know. I've never seen a trout do anything like that. But that reminds me—did I ever tell you about the time I saved a trout from drowning? The reason it reminds me is that I saw the trout bouncing and flopping along the bottom with the current. Good-sized brook trout. I caught up with him and netted him, and I discovered that he had a caddis case—you know, the protective covering that the caddis worm spins around himself, it looks kind of like a twig—well, he had one of these caddis cases, about an inch long, stuck between his upper and lower jaws. It was stuck in his small teeth, so he couldn't close his mouth, and if a trout can't close his mouth he can't filter oxygen through his gills, and he drowns. I took the caddis case out, and I put the trout in some shallow water, and pretty soon, proud as beans, he swam away."

Guy: "I was reading in some sporting magazine about a man who was fishing in a boat and he had his retriever dog with him, and as he made a cast he accidentally let go of the rod and it flew out into the lake, and the dog immediately jumped in after it, and he started swimming to shore and the lure was trailing in the water, and a fish hit the lure, and the dog kept on swimming, and he ran up on the shore and kept on running until he'd pulled the fish all the way out of the water."

Deren: "Could happen. Could happen. I remember once I was out in a boat casting a deer-hair bug for bass, and my leader was frayed, and when a big bass hit I broke the bug off in his mouth, so I put on a new leader and continued to fish, and then a couple of hours later I decided to quit fishing, and I was coming back to the dock, and suddenly there was an enormous splash next to the boat and this big bass came out of the water into the air and landed in the bottom of my boat. It was the same fish I'd hooked earlier—he still had my lure in his jaw. Of course, there's a simple explanation. The fish was jumping trying to throw the lure. He would probably have kept at it until he succeeded, but instead he landed in my boat."

Guy: "That doesn't surprise me. Did I ever tell you about the time . . ."

Other customers are men of considerable personal force, but when they come into Deren's shop Deren is sitting, they are standing; Deren knows where everything is, they don't; they are asking, he is telling.

After an exchange like "Hi, I'm looking for some leader sink," "Look on that shelf right next to you— no, not there, the other direction. Second shelf. *Second* shelf, that's the third shelf. Move that fly box. Look to the left of that. No, the left. That's the right. Move your hand back where it was going originally. Right there! Right there! It's right in front of you! Look right where your hand is! You're looking right at it," this particular type of customer's ears, having heard more sentences in the imperative mood in the last few seconds than they probably hear in a week, turn pink with embarrassment.

An important customer who has been coming in for many years, or an old fishing buddy, or a fellow angling expert, or any of the guys Deren has got to know over the years, he calls a son of a bitch. If the guy is present, he's "you son of a bitch"; if he's not, he's "that son of a bitch." Deren says the phrase with mastery, with delicate tonal shadings to indicate everything from a wonderful human being to a horrible human being. He says the phrase with the ease of a man turning into his driveway for the ten-thousandth time. When the subject of any one of these guys comes up, Deren will say, "*That* son of a bitch

—he'll never die, the Devil wouldn't have him."

—he tied saddle hackle on streamer flies with greater intensity than any man I ever knew."

—don't ever let him around a car, he'll destroy it in a second."

—he was a real screwball, a big, tall, good-looking guy. Slept with, lived with, married I don't know how many women."

—did you know he invented the après-ski boot?"

—I've seen drunks dive under the table when he appeared on the scene."

—he's a pinko crêpe-hanger of the first water."

—he married a girl in Greece."

—he's basically a correlator. He's not an originator. He doesn't have spontaneity. Spontaneity is what advances the sport."

—he fathered half the illegitimate children running around [a large American city]."

—he had a compass in his head."

—he would have made a great President but he wouldn't touch it."

—he could tie flies down to size 28 in his fingers without a vise."

—he was incredible. He'd make bets he could sight a rifle in to zero in three shots. And do it, too."

—he was always into me for something, as well as I knew him."

—he asked me to be the best man at his wedding, and when I got to the wedding he told me to put on my waders, and he was married in a pool on the Ausable River."

—he asked me to sign a bank note for him when he bought a new car, and then he skipped town, and I had to pay the bank, and meanwhile I'm getting these postcards from him, he's out in British Columbia, and he says he's having the best salmon fishing of his life and he wishes I was there!"

—he's a very enthusiastic angler. It's the Indian in him."

—forget it. He's a three-dollar bill. He'd write any kind of angling misinformation he could think of. He prostituted his sport for money. He's not a sports-man."

—he's an enthusiast of an extreme caliber. He won't eat, he won't sleep, he lives by the goddam tides. This lends him a cloak of irresponsibility, but he is responsible—to the striped bass. He was fishing on the bridge out at Jones Beach, which is illegal, and he had just hooked a big striper when the cops came along, so he jumped over the bridge and hung from the railing with one hand and held all his tackle and played the fish with the other until the cops went away. He's an angler at heart."

In Deren's world, an angler at heart is the best thing you can be. He describes many people as competent anglers or good anglers; he describes some as enthusiastic anglers; only a very few does he describe as anglers at heart. When I asked him what distinguishes the few anglers at heart from the fifty-four million other people who fish in this country, he said, "It's the call of the wild, the instinct of the hunt. It's a throwback to the forest primeval. It's the feeling of being in a state of grace in a magnificent outdoor cathedral. Either you have it or you don't—it's inborn. The first time I went into the woods, it was as if I had been there before." He looked at me significantly.

"You mean . . . like in a previous life?" I asked.

"Well, that would be stretching it. Let's just say I didn't have too many surprises. I could sit all day and watch a field mouse fifteen feet away, watch a bird in a tree huntin' bugs—sometimes they're comical as hell. People would say to me, 'What in the world do you do in the woods that long?' Well, Christ, you never run out of things to do in the woods. The woods are a constant unfolding story. But it wasn't the same if there was anything man-made in view. If you thought of man at all, it was a man who had gone through there silently. Maybe in some long-forgotten time an Indian who went to join his ancestors long before the Norsemen came to the American coast set foot on that same spot when he was following the buffalo. Or maybe it was pristine, the way the Lord of the cathedral made it. The romance of fishing isn't all just fish."

In *The Compleat Angler*, Izaak Walton says, "For Angling is somewhat like poetry, men are to be born so: I mean with inclinations to it, though both may be heightened by discourse and practice, but he that hopes to be a good Angler must not only bring an inquiring, searching, observing wit, but he must bring a large measure of hope and patience, and a love and propensity to the art itself; but having once got and practiced it, then doubt not but Angling will prove to be so pleasant that it will prove to be like virtue, a reward to itself."

More men than women fish. Sometimes this works out fine, but other times the shadow of angry excluded wives and girlfriends falls across the sport, and things get depressing. About women in angling, Deren says, "The Angler's Roost was the first place I know of that trained women. We pioneered in that field. A lot of women were getting fed up with this business of getting left home on the weekends, and so their husbands brought them to us and we trained them. Later on, the women we trained became the nucleus that infected a lot of other women. Of course, you had to indoctrinate them properly. Sit them on a rock and let the bugs chew them up and then ask them if they like it and you're going to get a negative answer. But if you can inculcate the angling mystique into them, you've got yourself a hell of a fishing partner. Some parts of some rivers had places where a female couldn't manage, and they needed different equipment sometimes, because their muscle structure is different from men's. But they became good casters easier than men, and they became experts with flytying and flies, because of their inherent gentility."

Deren's wife, Catherine, is a nice-looking woman, who was wearing slacks and a blouse and had her hair piled up in a bouffant hairdo the one time I saw her in the shop. She was as nice as pie to me then. Her perfume was unusual in that room filled with the smells of flytying cement, rubber, canvas, and True cigarette smoke. Another time, I saw her on the street, and she had just had some dental work done and she was really in pain and did not want to talk at all.

In *The Origins of Angling,* the author, John McDonald, says that angling existed in the ancient world, and that our knowledge of modern angling dates from 1496, when *A Treatyse of Fysshynge wyth an Angle,* by Dame Juliana Berners, was published in England. He says that hunting and falconry were the sports of medieval chivalry, that books on those sports had existed for centuries, that the publication of the *Treatyse* occurred at about the same time as the decline of chivalry, and that the *Treatyse* is addressed to all who are, in its words, "virtuous, gentle, and free-born," rather than just to the nobility. He says that it cannot be definitely proved that Dame Juliana Berners wrote the book, as people say, or that she was a nun, as people also say. He says that people fished with tackle that was basically the same as that described in the *Treatyse* until the eighteenth and nineteenth centuries, when the invention of a better reel, of upstream fishing, and of the trout fly that floated rather than sank changed the sport tremendously. He says that over the centuries there has been much argument about trout-fly patterns, that the *Treatyse* presented twelve trout flies, for the different months of the year, as if they stood for immutable truths, that these twelve ruled for a hundred and seventy-five years, until Charles Cotton's *Instructions How to Angle for a Trout or Grayling in a Clear Stream* introduced sixty-five new fly patterns, that in the eighteenth century Richard and Charles Bowlker entered the discussion with their *A Catalogue of Flies Seldom Found Useful to Fish With*, and that the dispute continues to the present. The idea is that some anglers like to use the flies that have always worked, while others like to experiment. McDonald says, "The trout fly is still subject to a constant pull between classicism and innovation. In recorded history, the score is now even: three dominantly classical centuries —the fifteenth, sixteenth, and eighteenth; and three innovating—the seventeenth, nineteenth, and twentieth."

So when Deren says, as he often does, "What in the hell is the point of using a famous fly that is some imported concoction from some Scottish salmon river which is probably the result of some guy having a couple of Martinis a hundred and fifty years ago, which doesn't look a thing like any insect on any stream in this country, and which never looked like any insect in the British Isles, either, when you can pick a bug off a rock and copy it and catch a fish?" he speaks in the voice of his century.

Much of angling today is disappointing. Some of the best trout streams in the country are now privately owned, and it costs twenty-five dollars per person for a day of fishing, and you have to get your reservations a long time in advance. The health advisory included in every copy of the fishing regulations for the state of Michigan says that because of the high PCB, PBB, and mercury content of fish from Lake Michigan, Lake Huron, and many of their tributary streams, no one should eat more than half a pound per week of fish caught in these waters, and pregnant women or women who one day expect to have children should not eat any at all. The acid rain that falls in the Catskill Mountains is bad for fish, so now fisheries biologists in New York State are trying to breed a strain of acid-resistant fish. In the absence of clean streams that are nearby and uncrowded and full of wild trout, the modern angler often concentrates on a particular aspect of his sport—one that does not require such a rare set of circumstances. Some people like to cast, and they become tournament casters; some people read about fishing all the time; some people write about it.

Deren concentrates on tackle, of course; he also concentrates on information. Information is vital to angling. The fact that anglers are always hungry for information is probably one of the reasons *The Compleat Angler* has gone through over three hundred editions since it first appeared. Anglers are always trying to find out how to fish, where to fish, when to fish, what to fish. They always want to know about new killer lures, new techniques, new hot spots nobody else knows. Nowadays, it is often easier to buy the most esoteric piece of equipment than it is to obtain a really great piece of information. An angling writer will tell about the tremendous fishing on some tremendous stream, and then add that he's not going to give the name or site of the stream, for fear that all his readers will go there and ruin it. Most angling information is subjective. A theory that one person puts into practice with confidence works fine for him but may be worse than useless to the person with no confidence in it—sort of like literature or medicine. Every angler knows one fishing secret that he thinks nobody else knows. One person will say he's just discovered the greatest fly or the greatest technique of all time, then another will come along and say it's the dumbest thing he's ever heard of, and so on. It is a cliché that fishermen are big liars, but some fishermen actually are. Sometimes the land of angling information is like that land in the riddle where half the inhabitants tell the truth all the time and the other half lie.

All day long, Deren hands out and receives angling information. People are eager to share with him the one thing they know. Sometimes he will throw cold water on them by giving them an answer that begins with his standard "That's one of the great misconceptions of fly-fishing." Sometimes (less often) he will tell them they are absolutely right. His agreement or disagreement is never less than vehement. A very large number of people, in his opinion, have no idea what they are talking about. He says, "You follow something long enough, and you realize you know as much as—or *more than*—anyone else, and that opens up a door. Most of this knowledge is based on having the problem yourself and solving it. A guy can come in here and ask me a question and I'll know I can answer his Questions 1, 2, and 3. But it might be two years before the guy comes in and asks Question No. 2." And when Deren is right (as he was when he told me how to catch a trout on that April day) he's really right. In the world of angling information, he gives the impression of knowing everything, and it is this impression that's important. If the stream of people who flow through New York bring Deren sustenance, then it is the weedy tangle of angling information, of statement and contradiction and myth and old wives' tale and supposition and theory and actual fact growing out of five hundred years of angling, that provides him with cover.

I have never fished with Deren, but once (although I did not know it at the time) I fished near Deren. One year, I fished in Montana for two months—mostly in the Yellowstone River, near the town of Livingston. Deren goes out to Montana in the early fall just about every year, so when I got back to New York I went to see him. I asked him if he'd ever been to Livingston. "You're goddam right I been to Livingston. I was hit by a truck in Livingston," he said. (He and his wife were in their camper, pulling into a gas station, when a kid in a pickup truck ran into them. He was not hurt, but his wife had to have her arm X-rayed. Nothing broken.) I asked him if he had ever fished at a place where I fished a lot, called the Sheep Mountain Fishing Access. "I remember smells, I remember the way things look, I remember sounds, but I don't remember names," he said. (I know this is true. Despite the fact that I have talked to him for many hours, and despite that fact that when I first introduced myself to him he said, "That's a good name for you," I doubt very much if Deren has any idea what my name is. But when I call him on the phone he always recognizes my voice right away.)

"Sheep Mountain is downstream from the bridge on the road that leads to White Sulphur Springs," I said. "The river breaks up into lots of channels there. There are a bunch of islands."

"Yeah, I know the place you're talking about. I've fished there. Not last time we were out. Last time, we camped on the river upstream from there."

"Just this fall?"

"Yeah. We got to the Yellowstone on October 10."

October 10 was my last full day in Montana. I fished all day, very hard, because I had not caught the fish I had dreamed I would catch out there. The river had filled up with mud and little pieces of moss right after I arrived, in mid-August—a man in a fishing-tackle store told me that a whole cliff had washed away in a rainstorm, up in Yellowstone Park, near the river's source—and it stayed muddy for several weeks. Then, after it cleared, the weather became hot and the water level dropped, and my luck stayed bad. I threw nymphs, among them Deren's big stone flies, and grasshopper imitations and bee imitations and ants and dragonflies all over the river every day. I caught whitefish and unimpressive trout. (Just before I left, I told that same man in the tackle store the size of the largest trout I'd caught during my stay, and he winced and went "Oooh!"—as if I had shown him a nasty bruise on my forehead.) On my last day, I took a lunch, drove to the fishing access, fished my way several miles upstream, crossed a bridge, and worked my way more than several miles back downstream. When I noticed that it was getting dark, I was on the opposite side of the river from my car, and miles from the bridge. I started through the brush back to the bridge. The beavers who live along the river cut saplings with their teeth at a forty-five-degree angle. These chisel-pointed saplings are unpleasant to fall on. The fishing net dangling from my belt wanted to stop and make friends with every tree branch in Montana. Occasionally, I would stop and swear for three or four minutes straight. At one of these swearing stops, I happened to look across the river, and I saw my car where I had parked it, lit up in the headlights of a passing car. I calculated: there was my car, just across the big, dark, cold Yellowstone; it was many more miles of underbrush to the bridge, and miles from the bridge back to the car; the river was down from its usual level, and I had forded it not far from this spot a few days before; but then that was during the day, and now I couldn't even see the other bank unless a car drove by. I waded in. I wasn't wearing waders. It took a second for the water to come through my shoes. It was cold. My pants ballooned around my shins. The water came past my knees, past my thighs. Then it got *really* cold. I was trying to keep my shoulders parallel to the flow of the river. The water came to my armpits, and my feet were tiptoeing along the pebbles on the river bottom. I still couldn't see the bank before me, and when I glanced behind me I couldn't see that bank, either. I was going downstream fast. Then I realized that, gathered up tight and holding my arms out of the water, I had not been breathing. I took a deep breath, then another, and another. When I did, I saw all around me, under my chin in the dark water, the reflections of many stars. The water was not getting any deeper. I was talking to myself in reassuring tones. Finally, the water began to get shallower. Then it got even shallower. Then I was strolling in ankle-deep water on a little shoal about a quarter mile downstream from my car. I walked up onto the bank and sang a couple of bars from "We Will Rock You," by Queen. Then I raised my arms and kissed my biceps. I walked to my car and drove back to the house I was staying in and took an Olympia beer out of the refrigerator and drank it. The motto of Olympia beer is "It's the Water." That night, I had a physical memory of the river. It was a feeling of powerful current pushing against my left side so insistently that I had to keep overcoming the illusion that I was about to be washed out of bed.

"Did you fish that day, on the tenth? How did you do?" I asked.

"Oh, that first day we were on the Yellowstone I hardly even got out of the camper," Deren said. "I was pooped from driving, and I honestly did not think that conditions were at all favorable. The water was down, it was too bright. I did take one walk down to the river, for the benefit of these two guys who were following me. When I'm in Montana, guys follow me wherever I go, because they think I'll lead them to good fishing. I showed these two guys a piece of holding water where they might find some big trout, and then I went back to the camper. Later that evening, after dark, the guys came to my camper, banged on the door, woke me and Catherine up. They had this goddam huge brown trout they'd caught, right where I told them. They were pretty happy about that."

"I didn't catch any big trout, but that same night I forded the river," I said.

Deren looked at me. "That's a big river," he said.

On the inside of the door to his shop, Deren has posted what is probably his most famous maxim: "There don't have to be a thousand fish in a river; let me locate a good one and I'll get a thousand dreams out of him before I catch him—and, if I catch him, I'll turn him loose."

For Larry Madison, a wildlife photographer and magazine editor who often fished with Deren thirty years ago, a thousand dreams were hundreds more than his patience could stand: "Jim would get in a pool and just pound it all day. I'd say, 'Oh, Christ, you been in there for ten hours and you haven't had a hit. Let's go home.' Not him."

Fishing is worth any amount of effort and any amount of expense to people who love it, because in the end you get such a large number of dreams per fish. You can dream about a fish for years before the one moment when your fly is in the right place, when something is about to happen, when you hold your breath and time expands like a bubble until suddenly fish and fisherman feel each other's live weight. And for a long time afterward the memory of that moment gives you something you can rest your mind on at night, just before sleep.

(Jim Deren died, and the Angler's Roost closed, in 1983.)

Nobody Better,
Better Than Nobody

❖

Poncé Cruse Evans, the woman who writes "Hints from Heloise," the syndicated household-hints column that appears in more than five hundred newspapers in twenty countries, has a cute nose and a cute smile and a strong chin that precedes her into confrontations with people who smoke in elevators and dry cleaners who ruin good silk blouses. On television (she often appears on talk shows, and forty-seven TV stations around the country use her minute-long household-hints tapes), her luxuriant head of completely gray hair catches the eye. She is only thirty-one years old. Her hair started turning gray when she was twelve, and she thinks that worry about her mother, who had many illnesses and died in 1977, made it turn grayer faster. Her gray hair and young face add to the confusion of people who expect her to be older and who are also not clear on the difference between her and her mother. Poncé's mother, Heloise, founded the column in 1959. Poncé began to write for the column occasionally under the name Heloise II in 1975, took over the column in 1977, and dropped the "II" in 1978. Her full name is Poncé Kiah Marchelle Heloise Cruse Evans. Poncé (pronounced *Pahn*-see) was the nickname of her paternal grandmother, Florence; it does not appear in the Dictionary of Common English First Names. Kiah is short for Hezekiah, a name of several uncles on her father's side. Marchelle comes from her father's first name, which is Marshal. Heloise is from her mother. Cruse was Poncé's last name before she married. Evans comes from her husband of two years, David Evans, a plumbing contractor.

When Poncé tells a story about a phone call between her and Joseph D'Angelo, the president of King Features Syndicate (her column makes more money than any other at King Features), she holds her right hand to her ear with index, middle, and ring finger bent and little finger and thumb extended, to represent a telephone. When she wants to express strong aversion, she closes her eyes, raises her thick, dark eyebrows, and turns the corners of her mouth down. When she describes how wonderful certain recipes are, she presses both hands to her breastbone, fingers spread. When she is mortified with embarrassment, she flops her head over onto the arm of the chair she is sitting in and stays like that for a minute or so. When she is having trouble with a door that is supposed to open inward but is stuck, she gives it a solid shot with her hip, like a basketball player throwing a hip check. When she realizes that someone she has just met is attempting a joke at an unexpected point in the conversation, she does a mild double take and then looks at the person as if the person were a common household object suddenly revealing a new and different use. Her regard is unusual, because whatever she looks at she looks at with one eye at a time.

"I'm an alternator," Poncé says. "That means I see with alternate eyes. I have no binocular vision and very little depth perception. Sometimes it freaks people out who ride with me, because I stay so far away from other cars, just to be on the safe side. I was born with a severe astigmatism. I'm talking about *kabongas!* My eyes were so crossed all you could see were the whites. When I was born, my mother was in labor for thirty-two hours, and the doctors said that maybe the pressure on my skull was what caused the condition. I had six operations to correct it. My mother promised God that if my astigmatism was cured she'd tithe her income to the blind, and He must've liked the deal, because the operations worked. Even today, ten to fifteen percent of the income from her estate goes to purchase Braille typewriters for children who cannot afford them. When I was on my book tour in Washington last April, I passed the hospital where I had the operations. I will always remember being in that hospital with my eyes bandaged shut, feeling totally vulnerable. When someone comes into the room, you don't know whether they've come to give you a shot, take your temperature, or give you ice cream. Listening to the hospital sounds—the cart rolling down the hall, cla-*klunk* cla-*klunk;* the bottles on the cart rattling; squeaky nurses' shoes; the sound effects of the cartoons on TV, like that weird bongo noise feet make when the guy runs; the sound of scissors cutting away tape. In the movies, they always show the doctors and nurses standing around the bed when they cut the bandage from the patient's eyes, but to be on the inside is really worse. It's probably because of that that I've had such acute hearing my whole life."

Poncé imitates sounds all the time when she talks. For example:

kneehhhh—Her hair dryer stuck on its lowest speed when she has just washed her hair and has to go on TV in half an hour.

sploof!—Baking soda coming out of the box all at once.

swt swt swt—Her mother making an abstract oil painting, applying the paint with clips from her hair.

ch-ch-ch-ch-ch-ch—Chinese people chopping vegetables.

chop chop chop—Americans chopping vegetables.

klonk! klonk!—Her father, six-two and two hundred pounds, taking a shower in a tiny shower stall with metal sides.

plunk!—Her pet macaw, Rocky, after being sprayed with a hose, falling from a tree where he had flown in an escape attempt.

ghhich!—Her father when he realized that the pilot of the plane he was boarding was a five-foot-tall woman.

Poncé lives outside San Antonio, Texas, and not long ago I drove down to see her and her husband. From Chicago to San Antonio, the road is basically one big strip. In Illinois, I passed a motor home with a large metal nameplate on the back saying *The Humberts*. When the combined Interstates 55 and 70 cross into Missouri at St. Louis, there is no sign on the bridge identifying the river underneath as the Mississippi. In Muskogee, Oklahoma—"a place where even squares can have a ball," according to Merle Haggard—I saw a Taco Hut, a Taco Bell, and a Taco Tico.

I drove around San Antonio for a long time looking for a motel. I wanted a locally owned one—the kind of motel that was built in the days when people thought owning a motel was a good way to get rich. Loop 410, the freeway that goes around San Antonio, is a circuit of more than fifty miles. The only motels I saw were the ones you usually see. Finally, driving around the side streets of a neighborhood sliced through with freeways near the center of the city, I saw out of the corner of my eye a motel that I will call the Miramar Motor Inn. I had seen no signs advertising it. It was on a street that dead-ended at a

fence along a freeway. On one side of the street it had
many rooms in cinder-block buildings surrounding a
large parking lot, and on the other side of the street
it had other buildings and more rooms. I went in and
registered, and after the woman behind the counter
took my money she asked, "How did you find out
about this motel?"

I had not been in Texas long before I started having millions of insights about the difference between
Texas and the rest of America. I was going to write
these insights down, but then I thought—Nahhh.

Poncé's mother, Heloise, was born in Fort Worth,
Texas, on May 4, 1919, to Mr. and Mrs. Charles
Bowles. She and her sister Louise were identical twins.
Heloise's mother was herself an identical twin, and
the day on which her daughters were born also happened to be her own birthday. As a girl, Heloise liked
to rub empty spools on the soap when she was in the
bath, and blow bubbles from the hole in the center
of the spool. She was interested in the Orient—an
interest encouraged and shared by her mother, who
gave Heloise and Louise matching Chinese cedar
chests for their sixteenth birthday. Heloise went to
public school in Fort Worth, and she was the only girl
in her high school to take shop class, and she got an
A in it. She also took private lessons in smoking, to
learn how to smoke a cigarette glamorously. She attended the Texas School of Fine Arts in 1938, and in

1939 she graduated from the Felt and Tarrent Business College and also from Draughn's Business College. In 1940, she married Adolph Risky, an Air Corps pilot. After two miscarriages, she thought that she could not have children, so she and her husband adopted a son, Louis. She and her son stayed in Texas when her husband went off to war. In 1943, he was shot down over Europe. Heloise received a flag and his medals in the mail, but she did not have enough money to go to Cambridge, England, where he was buried. (Thirty years later, on her only trip to Europe, she did visit the grave.)

In 1946, at a party in Fort Worth, Heloise met Marshal (Mike) Cruse, a captain in the Army Air Forces. He asked her out, and on their first date they went target shooting. They were married three weeks later, and they honeymooned in Mexico. Early in 1948, she and Louis went to join her husband in China, where he had been stationed. First, they lived in Shanghai and then they lived in Nanking. Heloise was both thrilled and horrified by China. In her book *Heloise in China,* written in 1948 (published in 1971), she said, "There are no words in the dictionary to describe this country and its people." She visited Peking, which she thought was the most beautiful and mysterious city in the world. Outside the wall of the Forbidden City, she saw many Communist students machine-gunned by Chinese Nationalist troops. She managed a household without a stove or heat or running water. She used rice water for starch, beet juice to dye clothes, and cabbage to clean rugs. She shot a .22 rifle to scare away Chinese people who broke down the bamboo fence around her house and began stealing clothes off the clothesline. She and her husband became friends with their upstairs neighbors, Major Les Garrigus and his wife, Helen, who were also from Texas. One day, Helen and Heloise made one huge Texas state flag and two smaller ones and hung them on the house, causing people to wonder what new embassy that might be. Another time, Helen and Heloise were going shopping and they saw a Chinese man raping a goat. This became a running joke between the couples, and in later years whenever they called each other long-distance they began the conversation by saying "Baa-baa-baa."

The Cruses left China in 1948, before the Communists took over, and moved to Waco, Texas, near where Captain Cruse was stationed. In the first five years of her second marriage, Heloise became pregnant five times. She always knew she was pregnant when she felt a strong urge to go out in the yard and suck rocks. All those five pregnancies ended in miscarriages. Finally, after a difficult pregnancy and a difficult labor, she gave birth to Poncé, on April 15, 1951. The Cruses moved from Waco to Arlington, Virginia, in 1953, and in 1958 they moved to Hawaii. In 1958, Heloise and her husband went to a party of Air Force people where everyone outranked them. The conversation turned to different ways to supplement service pensions after retirement. Heloise said that she would like to write a column in a newspaper to help housewives. A colonel laughed in her face and bet her a hundred to one she couldn't get a job on a newspaper. Heloise had some engraved calling cards made, and then she dressed in her best suit, with matching purse, hat, shoes, and gloves, and she went to the office of the *Honolulu Advertiser* when she knew the editor was out to lunch. She made sure she created quite a stir, and she left her card. Two days later, she went back, and this time a secretary gave her an appointment to see the editor. Heloise often dyed her hair offbeat colors; for the appointment she sprayed her hair silver. The editor asked her if she could type, and she said no. She told him her idea for a column and offered to work for free for thirty days. The editor decided to give her a chance, and she soon began a column called "Readers' Exchange."

At first, the column offered both practical and personal advice, but after a while the household hints that the column printed attracted the most attention. Once, Heloise printed a hint from a reader which said that Sanford's X-it, an ink eradicator, would remove banana-leaf stains, and all the Sanford's X-it in Hawaii sold out and a fresh planeload had to be flown in. Another time, she said that Hershey's cocoa butter was good for soothing rough hands, and the same thing happened. After the Honolulu *Advertiser* had been running the "Readers' Exchange" for less than three years, its circulation was up forty percent, and the editor said that it was mostly because of her. *Time*

printed an article on her and her column in June
of 1961, and Elwin Thompson, the editor at King
Features Syndicate, saw the article and suggested to
Heloise that she go into syndication. In September
of 1961, King Features began to distribute "Hints
from Heloise" nationally, and by April of 1962 the
column was appearing in a hundred and fifty-eight
papers. Her readership was so enthusiastic that when
she offered free to anyone who asked for it a booklet
about laundry that she had written she received two
hundred thousand requests—the largest delivery of
mail to an individual in the history of Hawaii. In
November of 1962, she published her first book,
Heloise's Housekeeping Hints. Early in 1963, the
Cruses moved back to Arlington, Virginia. In October of 1963, Heloise published her second book,
Heloise's Kitchen Hints. In 1964, at the Waldorf-
Astoria Hotel, she received the Silver Lady award
from an association of communications executives
called the Banshees, in recognition of her achievements as a columnist. By the end of 1964, her column
was appearing in five hundred and ninety-three newspapers, in America and foreign countries. The colonel
who had laughed at her at the party in Hawaii wrote
to her and asked how he could get a job.

For a long time, Heloise and her husband had been
looking for a place to move after he retired. They
wrote to chambers of commerce and considered many
cities all over the country. They wanted a place with
a good climate, low cost of living, good military hos-

pitals, and good mail service. San Antonio won out, and in 1966 the Cruses moved into a five-room apartment on Broadway, eighty blocks from downtown. They also rented an adjoining two-bedroom apartment, converted it into an office, and knocked out a wall in a closet so Heloise could go back and forth easily. The San Antonio *Light,* a newspaper that carried Heloise's column, sent a reporter named Marjorie Clapp to do a story about Heloise soon after the Cruses moved. Marjorie Clapp mainly wrote stories about medical science, and she was unhappy to be assigned to a celebrity interview. When she arrived at Heloise's apartment, she noticed that Heloise was barefoot and had blacked out several of her teeth with some kind of black gum. She also noticed that the closet that led to Heloise's office still had clothes hanging in it, and to get through she had to push the clothes aside. Marjorie Clapp was not surprised by Heloise's strange appearance or bowled over by Heloise's celebrity, and that pleased Heloise, and the two went on to become close friends. Not long after the Cruses moved to San Antonio, Heloise and her husband divorced. In December of 1970, Heloise remarried; her third husband was A. L. Reese, a Houston businessman and widower, whom she met while doing volunteer work with the Optimist Club. Heloise did not want to move to Houston, and Mr. Reese did not want to move to San Antonio, and so they divorced, and Heloise went back to calling herself Heloise Bowles, her maiden name.

Heloise had health problems her whole life. In addition to having seven miscarriages, she had a growth in her stomach (it was successfully removed), a disease of the heart carried by pigeons, tic douloureux (a nervous disease involving severe facial twitching and pain, sometimes leading to loss of consciousness), arteriosclerosis, and a cracked vertebra, suffered when a car she was riding in was struck by a drunk driver. (After the accident, Heloise sent state legislators letters printed on little Japanese fans saying that they should pass stricter laws against drunk drivers.) At one point when Heloise was very sick, Dr. Denton Cooley, the famous Houston heart specialist, told her he could help her if she agreed to stop smoking, and she said she just couldn't, and he said, "Then I can't help you," and walked out of the room. She planned her funeral over several years, with the help of Mr. and Mrs. Lelon Cude, a couple she met at a party. They visited many cemeteries shopping for burial plots. The Cudes (who owned a funeral parlor themselves) later remembered that at one cemetery she told the director in detail how to get rid of the anthills. She had picked a site, and had a tombstone carved and set up, by 1975. The tombstone read *Heloise, Every Housewife's Friend.* She died December 28, 1977, and was buried in a red silk Japanese wedding robe, which she had always worn on New Year's Eve. At her funeral, each mourner was given a long-stemmed red carnation, and a friend, Mrs. Paul Loomis, sang "There Are No Phones to

Heaven"—a song written and copyrighted by Heloise. Several obituaries recalled that she had liked unusual hair coloring, and these ended with a quotation taken from an official biography distributed by King Features Syndicate: "I just can't abide a dreary look, and when I wear a blue dress and blue shoes, why I'm going to have blue hair."

Poncé told me how to get to her house: "Come out San Pedro past the airport, which you can't miss because the planes land practically right on top of your car, get off at the Bitters Road exit, go left under the overpass, go straight through the light (if it's green, of course) . . ." I liked the last instruction, because it reminded me of the generous specificity of many of her household hints. For example, a hint telling how to polish sterling-silver bracelets by rubbing them on wool carpeting begins, "Remove the bracelets from your arm." Before I went, I put on a new pair of socks. These socks came on a sock hanger. This sock hanger was a single piece of molded silver plastic, about three and a half inches long and an inch and a half high. Essentially, it was a little clip with teeth to grip the socks and a hook at the top so the socks could hang on display at the store. It looked somehow special to me. I put it in my pocket and took it with me. When I was sitting in Poncé's living room talking to her, I remembered I had it, and I showed it to her.

She reacted like an Audubon Society member spotting an indigo bunting at her bird feeder. "Aren't those *neat*? You can do lots of things with those. They make great tie hangers or clothespins for dainty items like lingerie or clips to keep potato-chip bags shut after opening. You can clip matching socks together when you dry them (on medium heat), and that saves having to match socks later. Kids like 'em for clothes hangers for Barbie Doll clothes. This is the good kind, too—the teethy kind."

The good kind. Poncé knows that there are sock hangers without teeth, sock hangers of light-gauge plastic which break easily, sock hangers that are only a plastic ring with a tab that goes through the socks. She knows that the heavier-gauge sock hangers with the teeth—functional, eye-pleasing in design—are the good kind. Poncé knows about sock hangers because it is her job to know. Poncé's mother believed that homemakers were "the precious backbone of the world," and she saw significance in the smallest detail of a homemaker's life. Her vision, as she expressed it in her column, was so powerful that it gave her name a status bordering on the official. To many people, Heloise is a name like Aunt Jemima or Betty Crocker, and they are surprised to find out that there was an actual woman named Heloise. Poncé inherited not only her mother's name and her mother's column but also the vision that her mother shared with millions of readers. For most of the history of the column, about eighty percent of the hints have been ones submitted by readers (and tested by the "Hints from Heloise" staff). So many people participate in the column that the question of authorship is fuzzy: some hints readers send in, some Poncé thinks of, some her mother first came up with twenty years ago. But every hint is like another facet on the same crystal: "Hints from Heloise" will pick one item from the stream that sluices through our lives and then spotlight it, put it on a dais, examine its essence. A rubber crutch tip; a back scratcher; a skin-diving mask and snorkel; toy handcuffs; rubber fruit-jar rings; a shish-kebab skewer; a birthday-candle holder; a bowling-shoe bag; a nylon pastry brush; a Worcestershire-sauce bottle; a toy carpet sweeper; the skinny jar that olives come in; aquarium paint; a glass-doored china hutch; a thick book; a dresser scarf; the little piece of cork inside a soda-pop bottle cap; the square piece of sticky paper that covers the holes on a can of cleanser; a long-handled snow brush; a baby-food jar with a screw-type cap; a wire bicycle basket; a spice-bottle top; half a yardstick; the little circles of paper made by a hole puncher; a toy wagon. "Hints from Heloise" shows that these items are other than they appear. A back scratcher is perfect for cleaning the crevices behind the lint trap in an electric clothes dryer. Two rubber fruit-jar rings placed under an ice tray will prevent the tray from sticking to the bottom of the freezer compartment. Toy handcuffs can keep the cabinets under the kitchen sink shut, so crawling infants won't get into them. Thick books can weight down a towel blotting a stain from a carpet. If you wear a skin-diving face mask and snorkel when you peel onions, you won't cry.

When people complain that a hint in "Hints from Heloise" is sometimes more trouble than the problem it is intended to solve, they forget that just by naming the problem Heloise already has the battle practically won. Before "Hints from Heloise" noticed it, the problem of rump-sprung knit suits existed in the limbo of real but unnamed things. The problems of soiled artificial flowers, soggy undercrust, leaky milk cartons, sour dishrags, girdle stays jabbing, meringue weeping, soda straws sticking out of bag lunches, shower curtains flapping out of the tub, creases in the middle of the tablecloth sticking up, wet boxes in the laundry room, roach eggs in the refrigerator motor, shiny seam marks on the front of recently ironed ties, flyspecks on chandeliers, film on bathroom tiles, steam on bathroom mirrors, rust in Formica drainboards, road film on windshields—all were acknowledged and certified, probably for the first time ever, in "Hints from Heloise." Heloise was the first to call attention to the problem of unevenly distributed curtain gathers. Heloise observed that some things stick: zippers; car doors; bureau drawers; gum in kids' hair; toast in the toaster; plastic placemats to the tabletop; pieces of bacon to one another; one drinking glass inside another; envelopes to one another in humid weather. Other things slide: clothes to one end of the clothesline; purses and bags of groceries off car seats;

deviled eggs to one end of the serving tray; quilts off the bed; honeydew melons off the plate; sewing-machine foot controls across the floor; dog bowls across waxed kitchen floors; slipcovers off chair arms; sofa sections apart. "Hints from Heloise" noticed places that no one had officially noticed before: behind the radiator; under the bottom of the blender; between the door runners of sliding glass shower doors; between the little ridges on the bathroom scale; between the washing machine and the wall; between the stove and the countertop; where the grout meets the bathtub; where the carpeting meets the baseboard.

The intelligence at work in "Hints from Heloise" is confident. It likes to begin sentences with "Never," or sometimes with *"Never"* or "Never ever" or "Never, never, never" or "Don't ever, and I mean ever": "Never put any hot food into your freezer. . . . Never take anyone with you when shopping if you can possibly help it. . . . *Never* make one piecrust at a time. . . . Never walk down a long hall more often than necessary. . . . *Never* clean a closet or drawer when you are not angry or in the throwing-away mood. . . . Never walk into a room you are going to clean without a paper sack. . . . Never buy cheap paint for the kitchen. . . . *Never* wash windows when the sun is shining on them. . . . *Never* soak clothes over ten minutes. . . . Never iron a dish towel. . . . Never use bleach on treated cottons. . . . Never use scouring powders or bleaches on plastic cups. . . . *Never* sit, lie, or stretch out on concrete (that's cement) in any type of elasticized bathing suit. . . . Never buy shoes in the morning, because your feet *can* stretch as much as a half size by the afternoon. . . . Never put a rubber band around silverware. . . . Never use a perfume spray near silver, as perfume can mark it. . . . Never use ammonia on a mustard stain. . . . Never, never overwater a philodendron. . . . Never fill a dish to capacity. . . . Don't ever, and I mean ever, put hot grease down your sink drain. . . . Never, never, never use liquid dishwashing detergent in your clothes-washing machine. . . . Never run out of potatoes."

Although Heloise may congratulate herself and her readers for being "real smarties," she never wants to be mistaken for an intellectual. "I am no great brain, just a neighbor and friend," Heloise says. Sometimes the mathematics in the column seem to consist of one, two, three, four, five, six, seven, eight, nine, ten, eleven, a dozen, a bunch, two dozen, a whole bunch, oodles, umpteen, and a zillion. (Poncé, a business minor and a math major in college, once did a physics project on the rate of water loss from a dripping faucet and its effect on water bills. She is in fact very comfortable with numbers.) With its fondness for words like "thingamajig" and "doohickey," the column sometimes seems like the bright girl in class who hides her intelligence so people won't resent her; and, also like the bright girl, the column occasionally slips and uses a precise and abstruse word. Usually, it's a word that has to do with sewing, like selvage (the little strip at the edge of a piece of fabric which is of a different weave to prevent raveling) or rickrack (a flat braid woven in zigzags and used as a trimming) or flatfelled (sewn by placing one folded raw edge over the other and stitching on the wrong side, like the inside seam of a bluejean leg) or gimp (the round cord used as trimming on furniture).

Time has many rewards for regular readers of "Hints from Heloise." One year, Heloise discovers that a soap-filled steel-wool pad kept completely underwater will not rust for as long as two weeks. Several years later, with an intuitive leap, she discovers that rust on the cut side of lettuce leaves can be prevented the same way. One year, Heloise has a hint for "those of you troubled with 'lines' on husband's shirt collars" or for "women who complain about nylon slips clinging to their bodies." Years later, the problems of "ring around the collar" and "static cling" turn up on television. Heloise's readers never know when a simple one-paragraph hint in the column will predict a multimillion-dollar project involving soap-company executives, advertising writers, and TV-commercial directors, technicians, and actors.

In its early days, the column combined its hints with many encouraging words for housewives. Heloise not only noticed her readers' problems but also believed that her readers' husbands and children probably did not. She sometimes called her readers "my precious ladybugs," and she often ended the column "God bless you." Occasionally, out of the blue, she would say something that admitted how unrewarding the life of a housewife can be. She ended one hint about spring cleaning with the observation "All the furniture polish in the world won't put a gleam in your husband's eye!" When Poncé took over the column, she figured that homemakers were no longer only housewives but might also be men, grandparents, or even children, and she enlarged the column's focus to include them. "My precious ladybugs" disappeared. As if to compensate for the loss of that old camarade-rie, Poncé made the column much more down-home and folksy. Expressions like "Golly whoopers" and "Doggone and heck a mile" multiplied. She also put more emphasis on consumer advocacy and consumer safety. Poncé is less shy than her mother was, and she decided, with newspapers folding under her at an un-pleasant rate, that it might be a good idea to be on television. Over all, though, the column under Poncé and the column under her mother have been alike in more ways than they have differed. Nylon net—the product for which the first Heloise found so many uses that it is closely linked with her in the minds of many people—continues to divulge new applications. So does baking soda. So does vinegar—a substance that Poncé feels so strongly about that she flew to San Francisco to address the Vinegar Institute three days after her wedding. Poncé's mother thought that nylon net, baking soda, vinegar, and kerosene were the most important household aids of all. Poncé agrees, al-though she might replace kerosene with prewash laun-dry spray, since kerosene is now hard to find and prewash spray, a recent product, has a large number of uses, from removing bumper stickers to cleaning Naugahyde. She thinks she may write a book called *Nylon Net, Baking Soda, Vinegar, and Prewash Spray.*

After the first Heloise realized how powerful her column could be, she decided never to mention brand names. The second Heloise follows this rule. She calls Kleenex "facial tissue," Scotchgard "spray-type soil repellent," Clorox "a common household bleach," Kitty Litter "cat-box deodorizer," and Frisbees "flying-saucer-shaped toys." Not mentioning brand names is a good idea, because a really apt hint in "Hints from Heloise" provides an aesthetic thrill that, for a second, makes a person feel like more than just a shopper.

What actually happened was I got hardly any sleep at my motel, because someone kept slamming a door right next to my room all night, and then I got up in the morning and took my shirt off the hanger and a large cockroach jumped out of the shirt pocket and landed on the floor with a strangled cockroach yell. I drove out to David and Poncé's, and Poncé and I sat around and talked for a while, and then David said, "Let's eat." Poncé and I got in her Datsun 280 ZX, and David and Tom Carey, a partner in David's plumbing business, whose sister Sue was Poncé's college roommate and maid of honor, got in David's half-ton Ford pickup. We drove to a nearby restaurant called El Jarro, owned by Arthur Cerna, whose wife's uncle was married to Poncé's grandfather's sister and whose cousin was Poncé's mother's doctor. It was happy hour at El Jarro, where you got two drinks for every one you ordered, so the table was quickly covered with margarita glasses. Tom Carey said that sometimes when Poncé and David got into arguments he, Tom, would referee, and would jump in and yell, "Time out!" He asked me where I was staying and I said the Miramar and he'd never heard of it. Poncé said that she had had a dream the night before that she made David ten color-coordinated bibs with little clips on them like the clips on a dentist's bib, and she was so sure the dream was real that when she woke up she went looking for the bibs. I ordered the cabrito, which is goat, and a Carta Blanca beer, and they brought me two Carta Blanca beers. Poncé said, "Did you know that the Chinese have different sweat glands than we do?"

After lunch, Poncé picked up the check, and we went into the parking lot, which was very bright, and got in the car, whose seats were hot, and we drove back to Poncé and David's. Tom Carey got in his car and went somewhere, and I got in my van, and Poncé got in David's truck. I followed them into San Antonio on the freeway—everybody passed me because I was going only sixty—and at a stoplight David leaned over and lifted Poncé's sunglasses and looked at her. We went to a restaurant-bar named Yvan, where it was also happy hour. Poncé said, "Did you see they've invented a pill that you take and it tans you? Turns you kind of orange. Only problem is, it turns your palms orange, too." The bar filled with people, and Tom Carey showed up again. Poncé said, "Did you see that they've invented a flyswatter that looks like a little gun and the swatter shoots out and comes back?" Then the owner of the bar came over and talked to us. Tom Carey went somewhere again. Poncé said, "Do you *really* believe the Egyptians built the pyramids with wooden rollers?" Some guy with a beard came up to Poncé and asked her where she worked, and she said, "I'm a writer." He said, "You work for Ryder Trucks?" There was a lingerie show taking place in the bar, and models in nighties were walking around describing what they were wearing and how much the nighties cost. David said, "I don't like wishy-washy broads who say, 'Gee, maybe I will if you will, maybe I won't if you won't, oh, gee, I don't know.' Poncé isn't like that—she's not an easy woman." Then a model in a mostly see-through garment came up to David and said, "Hi, my name is Terri and I work for A Touch of Class Models and I'm wearing an apron-type baby-doll negligee from Shirlee of Hollywood and it just comes in red and the panties come with it and it ties in the back and it sells for thirty-nine dollars." David said, "I'm not interested in your body, I'm interested in your mind." Then we ate dinner and I don't remember what I had.

Next we drove to a place named Fuddruckers, and

there was only about a parking space and a half left in the lot, and David pulled his truck in and I backed my van really fast right next to him. We stood in the back room, at a bar that was a replica of an old Mexican tequila bar. When we came out into the parking lot, we were surprised to see there was only about a quarter inch between our vehicles. Then we went to a place called the S. K. Stampede, which was a dance bar in a shopping mall called the Central Park Mall, and David and Poncé left and went on home, and I tried to talk to a girl who was standing holding two drinks, and I bounced off as if she had an invisible shield around her. Everybody on the dance floor was dancing one huge synchronized Western dance, and I decided to go back to the motel. I walked out a door that I thought led to the parking lot but in fact led into the mall, which by this time was closed and empty and dimly lit. The door back to the bar had locked behind me, and all the racket in the bar was just a tiny noise through the door. I walked around the mall until I found a door to the parking lot, but the door was locked, so I walked to another door, but it was also locked. I sat down on the cool floor for a while. Then I stood up and examined the sliding security grate over a store window, and I noticed that the store had for sale a digital wristwatch with an alarm that played "The Yellow Rose of Texas." I thought about spending the night in the mall, and then I walked around some more. Down a corridor I heard voices, which turned out to belong to two jani-

tors, and one of them said he would take me to someone who had a key. He took me down another corridor and down a narrow hall that was completely dark
and through a door into a carpeted, track-lit office
with paintings on the wall, and he left. A member of
the Bexar County Sheriff's Department was in the
office, and he asked me for my driver's license. I told
him how I came out of the wrong door of the bar,
and he again asked for my license. I said all I wanted
to do was get out of the mall, and he told me to give
him my license and sit down and shut up or he'd
throw my ass in jail for public intoxication. I told him
I hadn't seen much else but public intoxication in
San Antonio that night, and his handcuffs made a
cricketlike sound as he took them off his belt. I gave
him my license. He asked me my birthday and I told
him. I looked several times at his name tag, which
said "Vela," and he asked me why I kept looking at
his name tag, and what I was thinking was, I thought
white people beat up on Mexicans in Texas, not the
other way around, but I didn't say that. Then I sat
there for forty minutes while he checked my I.D. with
the police computer, and when it didn't turn up any
criminal record he took me to a door to the parking
lot and told me that if it had been anyone but him
I'd be in the Bexar County jail right now. I took a
big roll of cash out of my pocket and said, "You think
I'm some kind of vagrant, but I've got over a thousand
dollars there." He said, "What motel are you staying
at?" I said the Miramar. He said, "Well, you better

not go flashing that money around the Miramar if you want to hang on to it." Then I got in my van and drove away.

The house that Poncé and David live in is 180 feet long. It is a contemporary-style ranch house, and Poncé and David designed and built it before they were married. It has two driveways. From the outside, at certain angles, it looks like acres and acres of blue clay-tile roof. At one end of the house, David and Poncé and Poncé's assistants have their offices. David runs his plumbing business from his office. The card catalogue in Poncé's assistants' office lists over fifty thousand household hints, with over two thousand cards just for nylon net. At the other end of the house is Poncé's bathroom, with a special deep drawer for electric curlers and hair dryers in the counter under the sink, and a scale set into the floor through the carpeting (because a scale won't weigh right if there's carpet under it), and a mirror with light bulbs around it, and a sunken marble bathtub with taps that look like golden shells, from which Poncé can look out the window and see the grove of cedar trees where her Chihuahua, Tequila, is buried. The other rooms in the house are a conference room next to her office, where Poncé can talk to people she doesn't want to bring into any other part of her home, and two guest bedrooms, a workroom, a den, four bathrooms, a dining room, a living room, a kitchen, a walk-in pantry, several walk-in closets, the master bedroom, a sauna, and a wine cellar. The wine cellar is a climate-controlled room, not a cellar. One of the guest rooms has a miniature bar in it. The living room is decorated with antique Chinese works of art—cloisonné incense burners, a temple table, an ivory ship with ivory figurines representing a Chinese version of the Atlantis story, and a folding screen with an ivory bas-relief of horses, which Poncé always liked as a little girl because one of the horses near the bottom of the screen has his legs backward. On one wall, there are opium bags embroidered with a tiny stitch called the blind stitch. Poncé said she'd heard that the blind stitch got its name because women went blind doing it, and that the Communist government made the stitch illegal when it took over. The living-room windows sometimes have feathery, sketchy body and wing prints made by Poncé's cockatiel, Fussy, when he gets out of his cage and flies around the house. These prints look pretty when the sun is right, and Poncé does not wash them off. In the hall by the living room hang two of Poncé's mother's paintings, *Euphoria* and *The Death of the Arizona*. The kitchen is futuristically spare, with vacant expanses of butcher block. Its simplicity is refined, like the simplicity of the ideal gentleman. It is latent with appliances; there is an electric trash compactor under the counter, and a microwave oven, two ranges, and two infrared food-warming lights. A blender and a toaster oven sit back against the wall, under quilted dustcovers. There is an extra spigot, and the water that comes out of it is 160 degrees. The decades that Poncé and her mother spent thinking about kitchens are palpable here. By the kitchen are sliding glass doors—with decals at both human and dog eye level to prevent collisions (a hint from years ago)—leading to the back-yard patio. In the patio are two Japanese pinball machines and a swimming pool.

Poncé: "I just love to sit by the pool and watch the roadrunners tease my little schnauzer, Zinfandel. They come up onto the patio as close as they dare, and when Zin can't stand it anymore she runs after them, yapping like mad, and the roadrunners take off, and then Zin gives up, and then pretty soon the roadrunners are back."

David: "That pool's just sitting there growing algae. I put half a gallon of muriatic acid in it and nothing happened. The problem was, a guy who worked for me left the filter on recycle instead of clean for four days, and we had a big rainstorm. Now I think we've got a kind of algae nothing will kill."

The San Antonio *Light*, in a front-page story about Poncé and David's wedding, said that a wedding guest said, "I've been in a lot of houses in Texas, but this is the first one that's in two time zones." The house feels that way not just because it's big. The sunlight ricocheting off the white driveways and the spicy breath of Mexico freshened through air-conditioning make most of the house feel like midafternoon in San Antonio, but the five or six hundred "Dear Heloise" letters that come to the office every day from all over the world bring that end of the house a much more dislocated sense of time. When the phone rings—with a discreet, understated, low-pitched ring that is somehow more compelling than a loud one—the call is often from New York, where it's an hour later, or Los Angeles, where it's two hours earlier. Poncé carries the phone with her on a long cord all over the house, and whenever the phone is, the feeling of abstract, average time floats above it. Poncé often answers the phone; when her assistants answer it, they tell her over the intercom who it is.

(*ring*)

"Poncé, a disc jockey from a station in Spokane, Washington, has a question for Heloise. He says the President of the United States is coming over to your house in five minutes, what do you do?"

"The President is coming in five minutes? Here?"

"No, no—he wants to know *what if* the President were coming over in five minutes, what would you do."

"My God, I thought he was coming here. O.K. . . . Hello. . . . Uh-huh. . . . Well, I would say first, pick up the big chunks. Hide the shoes. Stuff the dishes in the dishwasher, or put 'em in a tub and hide 'em in the oven. Open drawers and shove everything in off the countertops. Clean the bathroom mirror, make the bed. Then the house looks at least halfway decent.

Then sprinkle some cinnamon in a pan and put it on a burner on low. By the time the President gets there, the whole house will smell nice, like cinnamon rolls."

(*ring*)

"Poncé, a newspaper writer from New Jersey says she's doing an article on freezers, and she wants to know what you have in yours."

"O.K., thanks, Hazel. . . . Hello. . . . I know there's all kinds of things you can keep in your freezer, like sprinkled clothes before you iron them, or valuable papers so they won't burn up in a fire (in plastic bags, of course, so they won't get wet), or homemade labeled TV dinners in foil, or vegetable scraps to make stock, or popcorn so it'll stay fresh, or candles so they won't drip when they burn, or girdles so they'll go on easier and be cool in the summer, but, to be perfectly honest with you, what I've got in my freezer right now is just some old rolls to feed the birds, a couple cans of coffee, a few frozen pizzas, and something all wrapped in freezer paper that I don't even know what it is."

(*ring*)

"Poncé, a man from *Parade* magazine says he's doing an article on pet peeves, and he wants to know what Heloise's are."

"O.K. . . . Hello. . . . Well, let's see. People who come in and drop their purse and shoes in the living room. It only would take a second to put them away. Drivers who don't use their blinkers when they turn, or who keep their blinkers on after they turn. People who put out cigarettes in their food. Oh—you know what really drives me crazy? Wax for no-wax floors. Here somebody saves their money to buy a no-wax floor, and the next thing they know someone comes along and tells them that not only do they need wax for their no-wax floor, they need a special kind of wax. I think that's really a crock of cranberries."

Since being a homemaker and ordinary citizen is Poncé's profession, she can turn from Poncé into Heloise at any second. "I never realized what Heloise was," she says. "I've always made a point of being Poncé. To me, Mother was always just Mother. The first time she left Hawaii on business, I couldn't understand it. It made me physically sick. I was in third grade. I cried and cried. She said, 'I'm not leaving you.' Suddenly—boom!—she was gone. Now I realize how much it must have hurt *her*, and I realize how gutsy she was back when women were not. When she became Heloise, she had something to do most of the time—there were always fourteen jars of something she was testing on the kitchen table—so I learned how to take care of myself. That was good experience for what I do now. I started helping on the column when I was ten or eleven. One time, she and some neighbors and I baked two hundred loaves of bread about two hundred different ways to see which way of baking kept the tops the softest. I helped in her office, too, some summers. Other summers, I got summer jobs. Baskin-Robbins trained me for a week so I could scoop ice cream to just a certain number of ounces. I worked there for about two months and gained ten pounds and quit. Don't ever believe it when they say you'll get tired of the ice cream if you work there. Then after high school— I went to Alamo Heights High School, which was and is known as the snob school in San Antonio—Chris Geppert, who is now Christopher Cross, who's won four Grammys, was in my class—anyway, for a graduation present I got to go to Virginia, and from there some friends invited me to Ocean City, Maryland. One of those friends was Susan Dredge, who's now Susan Johnson, who lives in Hawaii, who invited us for a visit last fall. Anyway, in Ocean City I got a job in a Best Western hotel washing sheets and towels. When I went in for the job, the man there told me I was too short to fold the sheets without having them drag on the floor, so I went and found a wooden soda carton and told him I could stand on that, and he hired me. I got my best pair of cutoffs at that job—a maid found them in a room and gave them to me and they fit perfectly. The laundry room had no air-conditioning and very little ventilation and two commercial-size washers and one commercial-size dryer. I made seventy dollars for a seven-day week, and I learned quite a bit. My friends and I had a cabin across from the ocean near Phillips Crab House, which was always full of four hundred people knocking on crabs. I thought that was so barbaric. I also hated Maryland, because they had a state income tax. Mother kept writing and calling, telling me to come home, but I didn't want to. Finally, she said she was going to send the police after me, and

I knew she would do it. So she flew to Washington and I went and met her at her hotel, which happened to be the Watergate, and we flew back to San Antonio. That was the first time I was ever out of the state of Texas by myself.

"After I got back, I decided to go to Southwest Texas State University, at San Marcos—L.B.J.'s alma mater. I wasn't a sorority type. I don't need a sorority. I know that they're very beneficial, I just don't need them. I lived in a private dorm off campus with Sue Carey and two other girls. Sue and I have been best friends since high school. We never worried about stealing each other's men. We could wear each other's clothes—each other's tops, actually. I had a purple VW that was so neat, and I also rode a motor scooter and neither of my parents knew. Once, my motor scooter fell over and I couldn't get it back up, and I decided it was time to get rid of it. When it was my turn to do the shopping, I'd drive twenty-two miles to the Air Force commissary and shop there, because that was cheaper than driving all over town to five different stores. When people came over, they always opened the refrigerator and said, 'Gosh, this looks like my mother's refrigerator.' For my college-graduation present, I went to Russia with Daddy. Someone had put the wrong entry date on our passports, so the Russians locked us up at the airport for a day until they could find someone with the authority to change the date. I stopped eating beef after I went to Russia—it was like junior-high roast beef.

Over the next five years, I worked on the column, I took fencing lessons, I went to Europe three times, I went on a wine cruise, I went to China with Daddy. I would not trade my Russia or China experience for anything. I got a grasp of what it was to be an adult in an adult world. At the time, I would have traded it for a Thrifty Scot Motel. On January 8, 1977, when I was on a date with somebody else, I met David Evans at a friend's apartment, and then the next day, Super Bowl Sunday—the Raiders were playing the Vikings —I watched the game with him. Later, we went out to a bar, and David played 'Kaw-Liga,' that song about the wooden Indian, by Hank Williams, on the jukebox. That's when I knew David was a real San Antonio boy. I had several big arguments with Mother that year, because she was getting sicker and sicker and she kept right on smoking, but finally I accepted that smoking was what she wanted to do. Toward the end of 1977, Mother's health really declined. The day before Christmas, David and I kept trying to get her to go to the hospital, and she said, 'I am not going into the hospital on Christmas. I am not going to ruin your Christmas and I'm not going to ruin Dr. Hernandez's Christmas.' So David said, 'If you won't go, I'll carry you.' Well, Mother slept with a .32 revolver under the bed, and she pulled that revolver and she said, 'You lay a hand on me and I'll shoot holes in the ceiling.' "

(David: "I backed out of that bedroom pretty damn quick.")

"So she didn't go into the hospital until the day after Christmas, and two days after that she died. We were at the hospital. I cried and I hugged David and I hugged the doctor, and then I went and made phone calls. When I got home, I called Mother's friends at King Features."

Poncé believes that everyone is created equal. One of the first things she ever said to me was "There's nobody better than me, I'm no better than anybody else." Her mother believed that, too. She used to tell her readers, "There is no one who will ever come into your home who is more important and loved any more than your own family," and "I hope you will want to accept the facts and tell yourself that you are just one of the multitude. I am!" The readers knew that Heloise was sincere in offering each of them a share in the column, and that is probably why they sent in hints so willingly. For Poncé, the only problem with this egalitarian attitude is that, although she may be no better than anybody, she is both smarter and richer than most people. Her mother spent almost none of the income from the column, preferring to keep herself within the limits of her husband's service pay and pension. The column has been one of the most widely syndicated columns in the world for over twenty years. Now Poncé is in the same situation as a comedian who has become so famous making jokes about how girls put him down that he attracts all the girls anyone could want. She has been so successful understanding the life of the average home-maker that she is no longer an average homemaker —she is probably a millionaire. Poncé's mother solved the problem by slipping away from the name Heloise, as if it were a too crowded party in her honor. Poncé's mother's middle name was Kathy, and after Heloise became a well-known name she began to call herself Kathy. She had many friends—particularly at a vaca-tion spot in the Texas hill country where she had a cabin—who knew her only as Kathy and had no idea of her other identity. Maybe she anticipated that one day Poncé would have a similar problem, and that's why she gave Poncé so many names—so that she would have plenty of extras in case any one name became too famous.

When I was in San Antonio, I met several people besides Tom Carey and Officer Vela. I met Barry Byrne, Anne Cravens, Hazel Bolton, Anne Mundy, Bruce Lynxwiler, Milton Willmann, John Kungle, and Judy Hill. Barry Byrne is a pilot who met Poncé and David at a balloon meet. (Ballooning is a hobby that the three share.) Barry works for Mexicans who own private planes, and he was staying at the house while his plane was fitted with new radar equipment. Anne Cravens is a friend of Barry's who teaches deaf children in elementary school. She had just bought a new house in San Antonio, and her new next-door neighbor was harassing her at all hours by opening his windows and blowing an automobile horn that he had set up inside his house. Hazel Bolton and Anne Mundy are mother and daughter. They are Poncé's assistants. Bruce Lynxwiler is a handyman who at the time was doing some work for David. Milton Willmann is a well-groomed local policeman with heavy dark-rimmed glasses who stopped by Poncé and David's one afternoon on a social call. John Kungle is a police officer in Poncé's township who stopped me one night because the light over my rear license plate was burned out. Judy Hill knows Poncé from college, when she was one of her roommates senior year, and she came by when I was there. She grew up in Del Rio, Texas, and is a social worker for the state's Department of Human Resources.

I was talking to Poncé and David and I said something funny, and David looked at Poncé and said, "You know, we should get him together with James Reveley." James Reveley and his wife are good friends of theirs. James Reveley is a well-built, snub-nosed man with brown hair and a red beard who holds his elbow to his side when he talks and illustrates points with compact hand gestures. He has two professions —dentist and undertaker. As a dentist, he occasionally makes scary or funny-looking sets of false teeth for his friends. As an undertaker, he is something of a maverick. Other undertakers do not like it that he favors funerals that cost no more than five hundred dollars—a cause he once went on the Tomorrow show to espouse. He wears a beeper on his belt. We met him and his wife at Maggie's, which had an electric train on rails running above the bar. After some drinks, we decided to go to a restaurant called Texan Seafoods North. James Reveley said we should all go in his truck. His truck was a Chevy Suburban with dark-tinted side and rear windows. He and his wife got in front. David opened the back door, and we saw a cot inside.

"I think we'll take my truck," David said.

"C'mon, climb in," James Reveley said.

"What if you get a call on your beeper when we're at the restaurant? If we don't have David's truck, we'll be stranded," Poncé said.

"Nobody wants to ride with me," said James Reveley.

Poncé and David and I went in David's truck. "I hurt his feelings," David said. "I feel bad about that. But I couldn't sit on that cot."

"What if he got a call while we were at the restaurant? We'd be stranded," Poncé said.

Texas Seafoods North had a salad bar set up in the hull of a twelve-foot sailboat. "That's nothing," said James Reveley, who had quickly let bygones be bygones. "I was in a restaurant last week where they had a salad bar in a red M-G." We sat at the seafood bar and ordered shrimp and raw oysters. James Reveley called them "awsters." James Reveley asked me if the seafood wasn't better than they had in New York, and I agreed that it was very good. The restaurant owner came by (as owners tend to do when Poncé eats out). "We've got a man here from New York," James Reveley told the owner, "and he's been sittin' here just eatin' the hell out of these aw-sters."

Then he said, "You know, this part of Texas—Dallas–Fort Worth, San Antonio, Houston—it's got everything you could want. All over the country, people are starting to refer to this area as the Third Coast." He turned to me. "What motel are you staying at?" he asked.

I told him I was staying at the Miramar.

"The *Mira*-mar?" he said. "The *Mira*-mar?! You're *staying*—at—the—*MIRA*-mar?" (He gave the name an inflection unrepresented by any typeface.) "I cannot believe it! Don't you know about the Miramar? Haven't you ever heard about the Miramar?" He grabbed his wife. "Dear, this man is staying at the Miramar!"

"The *Mira*-mar!" she said. The two of them began to laugh so hard that they had to hold on to each other.

"My God!" James Reveley said. "The Miramar is the biggest damn rut hut in San Antonio!"

"Haven't you noticed all the traffic? Haven't you noticed the hookers all over the place?" asked his wife.

"Why, that's the busiest motel in town at lunch hour," said James Reveley. "You want to find a lawyer in San Antonio at lunch hour, go to the Miramar. There's a little barbecue place around the corner from the Miramar where they have great ribs, and if you ask a girl at lunch if she wants to go get some ribs most of them know that's just a code word for going to the Miramar, which is just a code word for shackin' up."

"The *Mira*-mar!" his wife said.

"I've got a macabre sense of humor," said James Reveley, "and there was a time when a buddy of mine and I used to put on dark suits and ties and sit in his black Plymouth on Miramar Street and scare the hell out of all the guys, who thought we were plainclothes cops. Those johns would start slinking around, we'd laugh to death. Listen, when you check out, don't turn in your key. A key from the Miramar —now, that's a real San Antonio keepsake."

Off and on for the rest of the evening, James Reveley or his wife would say "The *Mira*-mar!" and then all of us would laugh.

On Saturdays, Poncé's assistants don't come in to the office. The phone does not ring very much. Many of the rooms of the house are filled with the kind of midday twilight that goes well with the sound of someone vacuuming or the sound of a soap opera on TV. On a particular Saturday, Poncé woke up and exercised on the mini-trampoline in her bedroom. She made scrambled eggs and bacon and English muffins for herself and David. David asked her if she wanted to go to the big chili cook-off, the Chilympiad, up in San Marcos. She poured herself a Tab. I came over. We discussed the chili cook-off. Poncé said that the Chilympiad was interesting but in the last few years it had got so big that it was also a little sickening. Poncé poured me a root beer. David said he wanted to go up to Medina Lake and take his boat out, even though the wind was high and the lake was probably rougher than a cob. Poncé said she just wanted to stay around the house. She poured herself another Tab. David went to the lake. Poncé was walking around barefoot—the way she is most of the time when she's at home. She went out in the front yard to get the mail and play with her dog. She walked to the garage behind the house to show me the white 1972 Thunderbird her mother used to drive. It had only twenty thousand miles on it. She poured herself another Tab. She took an empty one-liter Coke bottle, soaked it in hot water, and removed the reinforced black plastic bottom. She punched some holes in the black plastic bottom with an icepick, put some potting soil in, and then used it to repot a several-month-old avocado plant. She washed her hands and fixed herself a cup of tea. She went to the workroom and caught her pet ferret, Fred. In the kitchen, she gave him a baking-soda bath, which she does often, because he is an albino and shows the dirt. She poured sploofs of baking soda on him and then brushed the baking soda out of his fur with an old, soft hairbrush. He lay quietly on his back during this. Then she tied a red ribbon around his neck and set him on the floor. She swept up the baking soda with a whisk broom.

She washed her hands again. She made lunch—a tuna-fish sandwich, Fritos, and a root beer for me, tuna-fish salad on lettuce and tea for her. She put the mayonnaise back in the refrigerator and then asked me if I'd like a pickle. I said yes, and she went to open the refrigerator. Her refrigerator is the kind that closes with a hiss as the rubber vacuum seal around the door sucks it shut, and then won't let go for thirty seconds, so that it is impossible to shut the door and immediately reopen it.

"Shoot," she said, and stood by the refrigerator door. The wasted seconds were almost visible, expiring in the air around her.

"Isn't there some kind of hint that would solve that problem?" I asked.

"No," she said. "There is absolutely nothing you can do about this at all."

Bear News

*I*n northwest Montana, in early spring, the frost-heaves and ice-cracks in the road multiply into pot-holes, and it becomes difficult to tell the many prudent drivers swerving to spare their axles from the many other drivers swerving because they are drunk. In the back roads, the frozen mud around the rocks and pebbles expands into larger circles as it thaws; then it turns to soup. Limbs of road-killed deer emerge from the melting snow berm that the plow left. Crows and ravens find them, and leave the scratchy calligraphy of their tracks clustered close around. Long lenticular clouds, as straight as a jet trail and as wide as a field, float above the foothills and next to the mountains. Other clouds come down the mountain valleys. From a distance, the valleys are a series of descending ridges, each darkened to a different shade by the density of mist it holds. People in forest management refer to these valleys as drainages, identifying each by the name of its central creek: the Birch Creek drainage, the Wolf Creek drainage, the Tuchuck Creek drainage. A drainage can contain thousands of acres, and in the almost uninterrupted fifty-mile-wide span of mountain wilderness extending a hundred and fifty miles south into Montana from the Canadian border—a region that includes Glacier National Park and several national forests—there are many thousands of drainages.

Sometimes camera crews shoot cigarette ads here or there in these mountains. Geologists working for Sun or Exxon or Arco come and go in helicopters, rocking the foundations with the *whump* of their seismic tests. During hunting season, wilderness outfitters lead clients and pack strings of horses and mules to backcountry camps. In the summer, hikers throng. Two years ago, Forest Service officials began to ask users of the Bob Marshall Wilderness Area to travel and camp in parties of no more than six; in that remote part of the Flathead National Forest, at least a day's journey from any paved road, foot and horse traffic had worn some of the trails to widths of ten feet. Certainly the mountains have been less wild recently than they were in past years. Still, there is an awful lot of forest and meadow and, particularly, snow-scoured rocky ridge back in there where nobody ever goes. If you stop at night on one of the roads that mark the edge of this wilderness and listen, the accumulated silence of all that empty space will break around your ears like surf.

Through the winter, possibly as many as six hundred and fifty grizzly bears sleep in these mountains, in dens dug, usually, at altitudes above six thousand feet. Sometimes as early as March, sometimes as late as May, they come out. One of my favorite signs of Montana spring is a short item that appears in one or another of the local newspapers:

BEARS START TO ROAM
GLACIER PARK—Bears are beginning to venture out of their winter dens, and several have been seen in and near the Park.

BEAR SIGHTING REPORTED
WEST GLACIER—Glacier National Park's first bear sighting of the spring occurred April 4 near the head of Kintla Lake.

GLACIER PARK REPORT
The grizzly are out! Glacier Park employees found the spring's first grizzly tracks this week.

In the months to come, I know, those tracks will fill up with bears, and the several bears will become dozens, and all the news stories with headlines like "MONTANANS CAUTIOUSLY OPTIMISTIC," "ECONOMISTS CAUTIOUS BUT OPTIMISTIC ABOUT MONTANA'S ECONOMY," "LENTIL GROWERS VOICE CAUTIOUS OPTIMISM" will have to compete for ink with the most popular topic in this part of the state—bear news.

Wildlife poachers who supply the Oriental trade on the West Coast and beyond kill black bears and collect the paws and gallbladders. The poachers sell the paws for twenty or thirty dollars each to a dealer, who sells them to Koreans, who skin them, bake them whole, and serve them as a delicacy, with a sweet-and-sour sauce. The gallbladders are sold as medicine: dried, powdered, and taken with tea, they are supposed to purify the blood. A frozen two-pound black-bear gallbladder retails in Hong Kong for about three thousand dollars. Other poachers collect grizzly-bear hides, teeth, and claws. Grizzly claws can be worth seventy-five dollars apiece, and the hide of an adult grizzly may bring fifteen thousand dollars. People who love to see animals in the wild collect bear sightings. Sometimes when one of them has been actually attacked while observing a bear, he declares himself pleased to have got such a close look. Bear biologists working for state universities, for state departments of fish and wildlife, for the National Park Service, for the Bureau of Indian Affairs, and for interagency research teams trap bears, inject them with tranquillizers, and then collect hair, blood, urine, tissue, and small premolar-tooth samples, as well as readings of blood pressure, pulse rate, and body temperature. From the samples, they collect data such as the level of epinephrine—a chemical that some biologists believe is linked with aggressiveness—in the blood.

The road I live on is called Bear Creek Road. Not far from my house I have found pyramidal piles of bear scat filled with chokecherry pits, and honeysuckle vines torn down like old prom decorations and trodden into bear tracks in the mud of spring seeps, and rocks the size of truck tires rolled out of the ground, and rotten deadfalls torn to powder. Once, I came upon a Western larch with the bark peeled in strips to a height of eight feet. Some of the strips were lying on the ground; others were still hanging from the trunk. On the white wood beneath were lots of vertical scrape marks, a few still oozing drops of fresh gum. A bear biologist has told me since that grizzly and black bears make those marks with their teeth as they scrape off and eat the soft cambium layer of the wood. Some of the tooth scrapes were seven feet off the ground. The only part of the bear which I have ever felt any urge to collect is the many bear stories that I clip and save from the local newspapers.

The first time I ever saw a bear in the wild, I was on my way back from fishing in a beaver meadow on state land next to the Flathead National Forest, about ten miles from the town of Bigfork, Montana. I was coming around a bend on an overgrown logging road when I saw up ahead a large black animal see me and duck into some thimbleberry bushes. I knew it was a bear. I didn't move and he didn't move for maybe three minutes. There was no likely tree nearby for me to climb. Then the bear hopped out of the bushes, took a look at me over his shoulder, and galloped like crazy down the trail. As he ran, his hind feet seemed to reach higher than his head. He splashed water up and made the rocks clack as he crossed a little creek, and then he went into the brush on the other side with a racket that sounded like a car crashing through there. For some reason, I picked up a rock. I felt the weight of the rock in my hand, I smelled the breath from a wild rosebush, I saw the sun on the tops of the mountains, I felt the clothes on my back. I felt like a man—skinny, bipedal, weak, slow, and basically kind of a silly idea. I felt as if I had eyes all over my head. I proceeded, a procession of feelings, down the trail where the bear had run. I saw the dark blots on the trail where he had splashed water from the creek. I kept saying, "A bear! I saw a bear!" I found myself looking over my shoulder for the instant-replay screen. I could not believe that this had happened and then gone by in a second, like trillions of completely unremarkable events. I quickly passed the spot where the bear had disappeared, and then I became happier and happier. I had just moved to Montana at the time, and did not know anyone there. I walked home through the charged twilight and went through the screen door and picked up the telephone and began to call my friends before I even took off my waders.

The bear I saw was probably a black. Black bears are smaller and more numerous than grizzly bears. Perhaps because there are more of them, blacks are more likely than grizzlies to damage property. They are less likely to damage people. Grizzlies have dish-shaped faces, and humps on their shoulders; blacks have longer faces, and no humps. A black will usually run from a grizzly, and blacks climb trees, perhaps because grizzlies, who have longer claws, usually don't.

If everyone in the United States decided tomorrow that bears, particularly grizzly bears, were a big nuisance and should be exterminated, they could be. An unlimited open hunting season, poisoned garbage dumps in the backcountry, and a liberal bounty system would no doubt bring about the end of the species in just a few years. In the past, people have made similar decisions about other creatures—cockroaches, for example, or rats, or coyotes. As it turned out, it was impossible to get rid of rats, cockroaches, or coyotes. Nature made them good at surviving in the world in whatever form they found it, and they continued to exist no matter how people felt about them.

An adult grizzly bear can dig up several acres of mountain meadow in an afternoon; can run through brush faster than a horse; can kill a twelve-hundred-pound steer. Often, a grizzly tries to adapt the world to himself, rather than vice versa. When people start moving into their neighborhoods, all the grizzlies don't retire quietly to the woodlot, like deer; some come out and tangle. They can make plenty of trouble, but they always lose in the long run. The only reason grizzly bears still exist in any numbers in the lower forty-eight states is that a while ago people decided not to see the man-bear battle through to the finish, and settled for a standoff in certain remote places. What this means is that ever since wildlife conservation has been a force in this country an odd extra dimension has been added to the environment where the bears live. Today, for grizzly bears to survive in the mountains of several Western states they must also survive in people's imaginations. If enough people could imagine a world without grizzlies, and could with equanimity dismiss the bears from their thoughts forever, then the bears' actual disappearance from the physical world would probably follow soon after. I like reading newspaper stories about bears because nowadays the newspaper is such a vital part of their range. There, and in magazines and on television, too, bears fatten on certain feelings people have for wilderness, and suffer for others. They seem to try so hard to remain living things in the midst of all the fantasies people have about them. A cockroach is mainly just a cockroach, a physical creature going about its business. A grizzly bear is also the idea of grizzly bears, the question of grizzly bears. In a way, a grizzly is as alive in the pages of a newspaper as he is walking through the trees from which the newspaper is made.

People who study bears have noticed that, like human beings, bears tend to specialize. One grizzly will become a skilled predator on elk, catching them even in the summer, when they are at their strongest; another will develop a method of fishing for spawning salmon which is all his own and involves peculiar headlong dives from the creek bank; another will be expert at finding the caches of whitebark-pine nuts which red squirrels make for the winter. Recently, when a problem bear was trapped and moved, a wildlife official explained, "The last thing the grizzly needs is more bad publicity." Every so often, a bear comes along whose particular gift is for publicity, and whose knowledge of the art, like a Hollywood agent's, seems to exist on a level way above good and bad.

In 1976, a bear began to appear in the newspapers so regularly that those weeks when he stayed out of trouble were news themselves. Soon the papers were calling him the Giefer Grizzly—after Giefer Creek, where he was trapped twice during a series of cabin break-ins. Wardens from the Montana Department of Fish, Wildlife, and Parks moved him many moun-

tains away both times they trapped him; once he
came back, and the next time he found his way to
the North Fork of the Flathead River, continuing all
the while to break and enter at a steady rate. The
wardens had fitted him with a radio collar, and one
day, while tracking him from an airplane, they noticed that the signal had stopped moving. When they
followed the signal, it led them to a broken-in cabin;
they found the collar lying on the floor. For months,
the bear strewed news stories behind him:

> Department officials have noted the bear is
> exceptionally smart about traps and snares and
> seems to be one step ahead of the wardens.

> Property damage continued to mount as the
> bear continued to damage cabins, even those
> well boarded up and offering no tempting
> food.

> An ice chest was carted outside, food
> smashed, and a screen door wrecked. Missing
> is a small stove.

> Larry Wilson, who owns a cabin just north
> of Trail Creek in the Flathead's North Fork,
> reported the large bear walked in the flour
> and "tracked all over the cabin; it looked as
> if he had taken a nap on the bed."

Extra wardens were added to the case, and local people began looking for the bear on their own. The Department of Fish, Wildlife, and Parks now wanted to take him alive and give him to the Bear Laboratory, in Churchill, Manitoba. There scientists would surgically implant a sensitive instrument beneath his hide to measure the reaction of his heart, his breathing, and his nervous system to different kinds of encounters with human beings. A group of professors and students of wildlife biology joined the chase, as well as a team from the U.S. Fish and Wildlife Animal Damage Control unit. On September 25, wardens thought they had trapped him, but it turned out they had a different bear (which later died, apparently of the dose of tranquillizer). The first snow came, and the Giefer Grizzly was still at large. Many people said that a cabin owner had shot the bear, and several claimed to have seen the bear dead. The possibility seemed so strong that some of the bear's admirers held a wake for him in a bar near the North Fork. Then, in late April of the following year, a supermarket owner and trophy hunter from McConnellsburg, Pennsylvania, named Ray Koontz shot an 800-pound male grizzly bear near Wigwam Creek, in British Columbia, about eight miles north of the Montana border, while on a guided hunt during Canada's grizzly-bear and black-bear hunting season. By the numbers on the ear tags, and a missing tooth that had been removed when wardens trapped him two summers before, the bear was identified as the Giefer Grizzly. His head, with the hide and claws, was sent to the Klineburger Brothers taxidermy studio, in Seattle, and the full-life mount was shipped back to Pennsylvania in a crate. The bear has since been displayed at several of Ray Koontz's IGA stores, and in the lobby of the First National Bank of McConnellsburg. Today, along with dozens of other mounted trophies taken all over the world, the Giefer Grizzly is in a room in the air-conditioned basement of Ray Koontz's house.

In fact, a bear in the newspapers is often a bear headed for a fall. Many bear stories follow a Watergate-like pattern, from the one-column item on page 6 to the sensational front-page spread months or years later. In late July of 1983, several papers reported that a 160-pound, three-year-old male grizzly had been trapped and relocated after eating dog food off a porch and killing domesticated rabbits near the town of Polebridge, Montana. The bear had been trapped and relocated once before, for similar offenses. This time, he had been taken to the headwaters of the Middle Fork of the Flathead River and released. On August 18, he was back in the news: he had been recaptured while going through picnic coolers at a family reunion on a campground on U.S. Highway 2 near the southern edge of Glacier Park, fourteen air miles and twenty-three road miles from the spot where he was dropped twenty-eight days earlier. The reports of this incident mentioned the bear's previous record, and added that the Department of Fish, Wildlife, and Parks had decided to turn the bear over to Dr. Charles Jonkel, a professor of wildlife biology at the University of Montana, in Missoula.

Dr. Jonkel is one of the world's leading experts on bears, and he has done a lot of work on the conditioning of bears through aversiveness training. In the past, he has successfully returned more than a dozen bears to the wild. For three weeks, Dr. Jonkel conditioned the bear to avoid people and food associated with people by blowing a boat horn and spraying him with a pepper-based dog repellent. After four months in isolation at the university laboratories, where he gained a hundred pounds eating rotten fruit and road-killed animals collected by Dr. Jonkel's staff, the bear was given a tranquillizer, put on a truck, driven about eighty miles northeast of Missoula, transferred to a sled, and towed by snowmobile to a man-made den above six thousand feet in the Mission Mountains. There Dr. Jonkel, his assistants, and officials from the Department of Fish, Wildlife, and Parks placed the bear on a bed of straw, covered the den with alder, willow, and pine boughs, and then piled on so much snow it looked like an igloo. "From the release point, the bear will be able to wander either into the heart of the Mission Mountains, or else east to the Bob Marshall Country," Mike Aderhold, regional information officer for the Department of Fish, Wildlife, and Parks, told a newspaperman hopefully.

When the bear woke up in the spring, he began to wander not deeper into the wilderness but nearer to people. On June 16, the signal from his radio collar was picked up at the north end of Seeley Lake, in the valley east of the Mission Mountains. At around two in the morning on June 20, the bear appeared in the yard of Roy and Kathy Burkhart, not far from Swan Lake, Montana. Roy Burkhart was away at the time; alone in the house with two small children, Kathy Burkhart watched the bear rush the cabin and get into the garbage and dog food. Then the bear tore the fence and the door off the henhouse and began to eat the chickens and young turkeys inside. She and her seven-year-old son, Forest, shouted at the bear, and Forest also shot at the bear with a BB gun. Then Kathy Burkhart called her nearest neighbor, Gordon Sellner, who was in bed and had the flu. Gordon Sellner got in his truck and came over. With his .25-06 rifle and a flashlight, he walked from the cabin down a path to the Swan River, where one of the Burkhart dogs was barking. The dog came running back up the trail, and then Gordon Sellner saw the bear walking right at him. He fired once and the bear fell dead. Afterward, a local game warden and an agent from the U.S. Fish and Wildlife Services investigated the shooting, and they charged Gordon Sellner with unlawful killing of a threatened species

—a misdemeanor punishable by a maximum $500 fine and six months in prison. A county judge later dismissed the charges. One of the news stories detailing these events ran a closeup photograph of the bear in life, looking at the camera from a patch of greenery with an expression as mild as Jim Lehrer's. The photograph had been taken by one of the game wardens who participated in the bear's capture the year before. It was reprinted courtesy of *Montana Outdoors;* two months before the bear was shot, his picture had been the magazine's cover.

The relationship between bears and photographers is a close one. If a grizzly is in camera range, he is both potentially dangerous and in danger. The photographer who takes a picture of a live grizzly one week may well snap the same bear dead the following week. Bears sometimes chase photographers up trees: in the foreground we see a pair of hiking boots, out of focus; in the background, some bark; and then (clear focus) a bear's claws, teeth, and blank, angry eyes. In other closeups, it is the bear who is at a disadvantage, lying spread-eagled and tranquillized on the ground with a researcher's bandanna over its eyes to keep the flies off, or hanging its claws through the mesh of a trap gate, or sprawled on the corrugated trap bottom, its fur matted with droppings and urine.

And when they are not in the picture themselves bears help photographers by showing them what to look at. Objects whose appearance has in some way been altered by a bear are, to judge from news photos, automatically interesting: a can of Sno-Seal waterproofing wax with bear tooth marks on it; an overturned outhouse covered with muddy paw prints; a metal garbage dumpster covered with muddy paw prints; a grove of lodgepole pines knocked down by a snared bear; a backpack with an aluminum support strut bent by a bear; a pile of ripped-up foam-rubber mattresses and a torn-open reinforced tent at a wilderness camp where, coincidentally, the CBS television newsman Robert Pierpoint and his family had once stayed five years previously; a barnyard littered with sheep carcasses; a plastic Little Playmate food cooler half torn to shreds when it was left overnight in the woods; a ransacked cherry orchard; a dug-up turnip garden; a chewed gunstock. Newspapers in Kalispell and Hungry Horse, Montana, once covered many columns with photographs of a campsite that a bear had raided. The pictures showed a crushed tent, some strewn clothes and personal belongings, a sleeping pad, an expanse of ground, and blurry trees; what set these pictures apart from the ordinary run of bear-damage shots was that they were also clues. Sometime after they were taken, the man who owned the camera was killed by a bear. The man was camping alone, and there were no witnesses to the attack. His remains were found in a willow thicket near the campsite. Authorities developed and studied the film in his camera, but in the end it told them nothing they didn't already know. A reader of the Hungry Horse *News* wrote in to say that he thought a bear could be seen in the top right-hand corner of one of the newspaper photos. That photo was further enlarged, revealing only pine boughs.

The man who owned the camera was named Laurence Gordon. He was thirty-two years old when the attack took place, in late September of 1980. He was from Dallas, Texas. After high school, he attended North Texas State University, left in 1970 to join the Army, flew a reconnaissance plane in Vietnam, returned to North Texas State, earned a degree in psychology, and became a commercial pilot, flying first for several cargo airlines and then for Metro Airlines, in Texas. April 21, 1978, was a date he considered important in his life, because that was when he met the Reverend John Samson, of Brighton, England, in the Dallas–Fort Worth Airport. The two discussed religion and exchanged religious readings. In May of 1978, Gordon quit his job, and he made trips to England to visit Reverend Samson that month and the next. In September, Gordon visited Reverend Samson in Israel, where he was teaching, and took a three-month course in Hebrew, so he could read the Old Testament in the original. After Gordon returned to the United States, he stayed with his mother in Dallas for a few months, and then began hitchhiking around the country with only a backpack and a cedar walking stick. For a while, he worked at the Camlu Retirement Apartments, in Pendleton,

Oregon. Gordon often talked to people he met in his travels about Jesus Christ, and he so impressed the Bill Crockford family, of Cut Bank, Montana, that they invited him to stay at their house. "His love of the Lord just radiated out of him—he had the sort of thing good Christians strive for," Bill Crockford said later. It was from the Crockfords' that Gordon went to Glacier Park and then hiked to a campsite at the foot of Elizabeth Lake. He and Reverend Samson, who was also traveling in the United States, had agreed to meet in a priory in Vermont on October 3, 1980. Reverend Samson was sitting alone in the chapel before the evening service when he suddenly felt a strong presence, turned around, saw no one, and knew that Larry was with him. Two weeks after the attack, a Glacier Park ranger named Jerry DeSanto shot a six-year-old male grizzly on the shore of Helen Lake, about four miles from the attack site; the bear was never positively identified as the one responsible, although its canine teeth closely matched bite marks on a daily scriptural companion found at Gordon's campsite. In the willow thicket the bear had left nothing of Laurence Gordon but a pelvic bone, two leg bones, a completely cleaned skull, and two hiking boots, which appeared to have been peeled off like banana skins.

Two years later, Glacier Park officials released a study done by a bear-management ranger of bear incidents in the park from 1967 to 1982. The study included a list of campsites on a chart showing the "Estimated Camper Use Days 1967–1982," "Total Bear Incidents" (those involving property damage or personal injury), and "Estimated Risk" for each campground. Campers used the site at the foot of Elizabeth Lake, where Laurence Gordon died, an estimated 21,339 days during those years and suffered a total of four bear incidents. Dividing the second number by the first, the study came up with an "Estimated Risk" for that campground of .0002.

Recently, I spent an afternoon tracking three bears along the side of a mountain just above the snow line. A bear track has an ovoid, palm-shaped print at the center and, above that, five toe prints, with a pointy hole made by the claw above each toe. The hind-foot track of the biggest bear was the size of a squash racquet. I have tried before to track elk, deer, and rabbits, but those animals all seem to wander around at random, and are about as much fun to follow as flies. The bear tracks took an even straighter path than a man would. The big bear went through thick brush without breaking stride or putting its foot differently. The smaller sets of tracks—cubs', probably —went off on skidding tangents and curlicues but always returned to parallel the big set of tracks. Of course, I was following the tracks not forward but back, in the direction they came from. If these were grizzlies, I did not want to come upon a mother with cubs. The time was late April, and I was hoping I might end up at the den the bears had just left; then I could stick my nose inside and find out what bears smell like. When I came around to the sunny side of the mountain, the snow disappeared, and I lost the trail. From this height, the bears could see farmhouses, and fields of Christmas trees in rows, and trucks, and mercury blobs of ponds, and the red lights of a motel sign, and roads stretching west across the Flathead Valley. They could hear distant hammering, and dogs barking, and chain saws. They could probably smell the steaks on a barbecue grill in the development a couple of thousand feet below them, and the vacuuming as a man cleaned out his car. What I admired about the tracks was how much restraint and purpose they showed. They were like a dotted line drawn on the mountain marking the farthest boundary of the land where it was sensible for bears to live.

About two million people visit Glacier Park every year. Only a few of them ever even see a bear. During the period 1975 to 1984, a hundred and thirty-nine park visitors reported that bears had damaged their gear, twenty people were injured by bears, and four people were killed by bears. Beth Ladeau, the park's librarian, answers ten thousand letters every year from people who want vacation information. Many of them are worried about meeting up with a bear.

Some are so scared that they call Beth Ladeau on the phone. Beth Ladeau often tells these people that they are much more likely to get hurt in their cars driving to the park than they are to get hurt by a bear inside the park.

Somehow, a car accident doesn't have the same effect on the imagination that a bear attack has. Car accidents are familiar and man-made; bear attacks seem to come from someplace else. Many of the people who write to Beth Ladeau have heard of Bear No. 15. No. 15 is perhaps the best-known bear of recent history. Biologists studying grizzlies in the area of Yellowstone National Park gave No. 15 his name when he was five years old. By the time No. 15 was twelve, he had been trapped more than twenty times, had been fitted with a variety of radio collars, and had been the subject of part of a master's thesis in wildlife biology at Montana State University. Over the years, an interagency study team set up in 1974 to keep track of the status of grizzlies spent more time observing No. 15 than any other bear. The biologists had always considered No. 15 a good bear, and they felt safe with him. One night in June of 1983, No. 15 tore through a tent in the Rainbow Point Campground in the Gallatin National Forest, just west of Yellowstone, dragged a man out, and killed and partly ate him. Within hours of the killing, a board of inquiry began to study it. Experts on the subject often say that bears are unpredictable, but the way

the experts investigate serious bear attacks shows that
they really hope for rational explanations of anything
a bear may do. Sometimes this makes them take a
harder look at the victim than even a heavenly jury
would. No. 15's victim had followed the rules for safe
camping in bear country: he and a companion had
locked their food in the car, cooked some distance
from the tent, and washed their dishes after they ate.
Having noted all that, the board of inquiry reported
in November that it could find no certain reason for
the attack. The board did add, among other possible,
unprovable reasons, the fact that the victim had been
wearing a strong-smelling foot medication at the time
and the fact that his sleeping bag was "fairly dirty."

No. 15, who was killed by a lethal injection the day
after the attack, went on to figure in news stories
about grizzly bears in many local papers, on national
television, and in the London *Times*. Some writers
suggested that No. 15's brain had been affected by the
tranquillizer Sernylan, which had been used on No. 15
maybe eleven times in his life, and which contains
the hallucinogen phencyclidine hydrochloride—PCP,
sometimes called angel dust. A number of bear experts then disputed this theory. As the discussion
about No. 15 continued, the bear began to seem more
like a personality or a celebrity, and less like an animal. The Billings, Montana, *Gazette* called No. 15's
attack "an irrational act."

Many other people who write to Beth Ladeau ask
about the events of August 13, 1967. ("They are never

going to let us forget August 13," Beth Ladeau says.) Early that morning, two young women became the first people killed by bear attack in the fifty-seven-year history of Glacier Park. Both young women were nineteen-year-old college sophomores with summer jobs in the park. Both decided to go camping with friends on August 12. They were killed within a few hours of each other, at campsites miles apart, by two different bears. The events of that night became the basis of a good book (*The Night of the Grizzlies*, by Jack Olsen) and more news coverage than Glacier Park had ever had before. August 13 also led to a complete change in the park's bear-management policies. Rangers began to shoot bears the second time they misbehaved, and new regulations tried to keep human food and garbage away from bears. One of the killer bears had been fed by campers in the past and had spent that summer chasing people up trees and raiding packs; the other may have lost the fear of man as a result of eating table scraps that were dumped every night behind a park chalet to attract grizzlies for guests to watch. Why both bears chose the same night to break a fifty-seven-year pattern of truce is unknown.

Bear attacks seem to run in twos, and often have a strange geminate quality. In 1980, two more Glacier Park employees were attacked and killed while camping; one of them was the brother of a seasonal biologist for the park who had been mauled by a grizzly sow the summer before. The chances of any one person's being attacked by a grizzly are certainly small; the chances of its happening at different times to two members of one family must be infinitesimal. Several summers after shooting the bear suspected in the death of Laurence Gordon, Glacier Park Ranger Jerry DeSanto was himself attacked by a grizzly. He was alone on his regular foot patrol in the northern part of the park when he saw a grizzly sow and two cubs about sixty yards up the trail. He left the trail and climbed a tree. The sow came climbing after him, pulled off his shoe, bit his leg, pulled him to the ground, and then bit him some more. Ranger DeSanto said that while the bear was on top of him "I cussed at her and hit her in the face with my pack." Six weeks later, two hikers were coming down Elk Mountain, near the park's southern tip, when they, too, saw a sow grizzly with cubs and began to climb trees. The bear chased one of the hikers, a man named Richard Kirchhoffer, and pulled him down. He later said that while the bear was pulling at him "I kicked the bear, spoke strong words to it." (Kirchhoffer at the time was the pastor of two Episcopal churches in the area.) In September of 1983, a bear came charging out of a snowstorm on the Crypt Lake Trail, in Waterton Lakes National Park, just across the Canadian border from Glacier, and attacked a young couple from Calgary who were hiking out after an overnight trip. Both the man and the woman were severely bitten on the face and head. The following September, another couple were attacked, this time near a back-country campground in Glacier's Fifty Mountain area. They were from Atherton, California, and had decided to visit the park after reading an article about it in *Outside*. The woman, Frances Lordan, who was a makeup artist and occasional model, described how the bear came growling, panting, and gnashing its teeth, and how the bear's hind legs skidded under it as it pivoted to chase her companion. She said that the bear pushed her down as she was running for a climbable tree, and that she watched the bear take a bite out of her thigh and swallow it. Frances Lordan and her companion have since hired the office of the attorney Melvin Belli to sue the federal government for not providing adequate warning of the danger from bears in Glacier Park.

It may be that people who are interested in medical science are more likely than the average person to want to hike and camp in the Northern Rockies. Whatever the reason, an unusual number of surgeons, associate professors of medicine, registered nurses, interns, medical students, dental students, emergency medical technicians, postdoctoral trainees in medical genetics, and students of acupuncture and Oriental medicine turn up in the reports of bear encounters through the years. The bear story that sticks foremost in my mind involved a young Glacier Park road patrolman and registered emergency medical technician named Gary Brogdon. In the late summer of 1983, Gary Brogdon was hiking on the park's Iceberg Lake Trail with his wife and baby daughter when a grizzly burst from the brush and charged them. Mrs. Brogdon, who was carrying the baby on her back in a baby pack, dived off the trail under some bushes, and Gary Brogdon lay down and played dead. Then he heard the sound of the bear's teeth snapping, thought it was attacking the baby, and jumped up. The bear ran up the trail, then charged back, snapped at the baby, and began spinning in circles, making noise, and kicking up dust. Then Gary Brogdon yelled and the bear ran off. The whole encounter lasted less than a minute. The baby slept through it. A local newspaper reported the story on page 1; as the paper reminded readers (although close followers of bear news should have remembered), Gary Brogdon was the same man who, back in May, was helping a ranger to transport a thirty-pound female black-bear cub that had been hanging around a park road when the cub stopped breathing after the dose of tranquillizers. That incident also made the front page; adapting his E.M.T. training to the situation, Gary Brogdon had sealed the cub's lips with his hands, and started blowing down the cub's nose. He could feel the cub's lungs inflating. After about three minutes, the cub took a breath on her own, and she soon recovered. Gary Brogdon, who with his wife and daughter escaped a charging grizzly unharmed, also happened to be the only man ever to save a bear's life by mouth-to-nose resuscitation.

Some letters to the editor:

I say let the grizzly bears and wolves go with the dinosaurs and saber-toothed tigers. These animals have been gone for millions of years and the world is still turning.

What the hell do people think that park was put there for! It sure wasn't for people! It was to preserve those beautiful animals and they sure can't be preserved if every time those rangers turn around they are faced with people who don't even belong there.

How many grizzly bears does Mr. —— want? Does he think they should outnumber the people in this area? . . . What about the people who depend on this area for their livelihood? . . . Jobs! Homes! Security! For myself and hundreds of others. These would all be wiped out—all for the GRIZZLY!!

If you don't like the grizzlies, stay away from their habitat.

I have a friendly relationship with a cinnamon bear and her family in the South Fork that has lasted for several years. Not once have they attacked me.

In regard to the selfish, greedy, idiotic letter you received from —— on the grizzly problem in the park. Let me say this, Mr. —— . . . I would be ashamed to class myself

as a man if I had anything to do with a situa-
ation as you suggest (demand our congress-
men to quash the endangered species, namely
the grizzly bear). It's people like you who need
quashing.

Newspapers in Montana never seem to run letters
from people who say they have no opinion at all
about grizzly bears. This may be because practically
nobody in the state old enough to write is without
strong feelings on the subject. I am no different: I
think that the problems that occur between people
and bears are made a lot worse by the tendency of
people to regard each other as a kind of virus. I think
that this tendency really bloomed in the late nineteen-
sixties, and that it is still around. People describe each
other in terms of the twenty-six-foot Winnebago motor homes complete with stove, shower, color TV,
hidden wall safe, and six lawn chairs strapped on the
back which some of us use to enjoy nature when we
go to a national park. Or else they describe each other
in terms of backpacks and granola and designer hiking
shoes and ten-dollar-a-serving foil envelopes of freeze-
dried gourmet trail food. Sometimes when you ask a
park ranger a question, you see reflected in her face
not yourself but the Public—just another of two million units rolling in from the conveyor belt of the
highway.

I believe that sometimes bears can read people's
minds. If you hike three miles up a steep grade with a

heavy pack for an hour and a half on a trail closed to all vehicles and when you're almost at the top a person on a knobby-tire motorcycle burns by you and then, a little ways ahead, stops, sets his kickstand, and lights a cigarette, chances are that you will have a violent thought about that person. I believe that the thought hangs in the air after you leave, and that a bear may absorb it, and use it in his own way.

I also believe that bears are very formal. I think that protocol is a comfort to them. Glacier Park recommends that hikers in bear country use bear bells —bells worn to jingle at each step, to let the bears know that someone's coming. In the history of the park, only one hiker using a bear bell has ever been attacked, and that hiker was near a noisy creek. I think that when we're in the woods bears want to know what we're doing. So I think we should try and know better what we're doing ourselves. Biologists spend lifetimes studying bears; people who visit the parks should occasionally study each other. Bears can't talk, but people can. Knowing that a person drives a Winnebago or eats granola is not enough. Divided up into "types," we will never have real dominion over the bears. All we will be able to manage, finally, is a disorderly retreat or a slaughter.

The day after I saw my first bear in the wild, I saw my second, third, and fourth bears. I was out fishing again, trying to get to an oxbow lake near my house, which was mostly surrounded by fences and "Posted" signs. On the one unfenced side of the lake, a pine and fir forest descended to a marsh, with little trickling creeks, and hip-deep black muck holes with oily films on top, and stands of yellow skunk cabbage, and downed trees with their roots full of dried mud sticking high in the air. I was coming through a thick willow grove when I heard a single woof, as distinct as a word. I thought it might be a deer snorting, but then through the leaves I saw two brown shapes climbing a cottonwood tree. I pushed the willows aside just in time to see a big black bear go right up the trunk. The bear did not climb putting one foot here and one foot there; she shot up with her belly flat to the trunk, her four legs rowing in a blur and throwing off bark chips. She went up in a second, as if on rails. When she reached a fork in the tree, she leaned her back against one branch and put her feet on the other branch. I took a step closer, and she woofed again, at the cubs invisible above her, and I could hear them climb some more. She was by far the biggest thing I'd ever seen in a tree. I looked and blinked and looked and blinked. Her fur had whorls, and tufts, and smooth places, and it seemed to be wrist-deep. Mule deer are the color of pine trunks in winter light; elk have on their necks the dark brown of wet bark and on their sides the golden tint of sun on a bare hill. This bear's fur was the smoky blue-black of night when it starts to fill a pine forest. Her snout moved back and forth in short arcs, and she watched me out of the corner of her eye.

I detoured around the tree. A couple of hundred yards away, I looked back, and saw the two cubs high on a limb, in the green sunlight coming through the new cottonwood leaves. The lower cub was trying to back down, and the one above was going head first. They were nose to nose, and vexed. I heard a rush of scrabbling sound as the big bear came down the tree below them. The cubs kept craning their heads around, trying to see where they were going, and grabbing and regrabbing the bark with their spread claws. My stomach growled, and I jumped about a foot.

It is possible to walk for a long time in the woods and not see much of anything. Beautiful scenery makes its point quickly; then you have to pay attention, or it starts to slide by like a loop of background on a Saturday-morning cartoon. A pinecone falls from one limb to another, a rock clatters down a canyon, and your own thoughts talk on inside your head. People sometimes say that what is great about bears, and especially grizzlies, is the large tracts of wilderness they imply—that a good bear population indicates a healthy, unspoiled habitat. But bears don't simply imply wilderness—bears are wilderness. Bear is what all the trees and rocks and meadows and mountains and drainages must add up to. When you see a bear, the spot where you see it becomes instantly different from every place else you've seen. Bears make you pay attention. They keep the mountains from turning into a blur, and they stop your self from bullying you like nothing else in nature. A woods with a bear in it is real to a man walking through it in a way that a woods with no bear is not. Roscoe Black, a man who survived a serious attack by a grizzly in Glacier Park several years ago, described the moment when the bear had him on the ground: "He laid on me for a few seconds, not doing anything . . . I could feel his heart beating against my heart." The idea of that heart beating someplace just the other side of ours is what makes people read about bears and tell stories about bears and theorize about bears and argue about bears and dream about bears. Bears are one of the places in the world where big mysteries run close to the surface.

Komar and Melamid

Two guys I wanted very much to like me are
the Russian conceptual artists Vitaly Komar and
Alexander Melamid. Vitaly Komar is heavyset, with
horn-rimmed glasses and dark Tartar curls and a
smile sparked with gold dental work. At doorways,
with a brief and accurate bow he allows his compan-
ions to go first. He is a veteran of one year's service in
the Soviet Army, where he painted signs and posters
and hundreds of portraits of Nikita Khrushchev.
Sometimes, for fun, he clasps his hands over his knit
vest, fills his eyes with spurious warmth, and imitates
a Russian policeman saying, "Dear citizens, *hhhhhow*
can I *hhhhhelp* you?"

His partner, Alexander Melamid (the two began
working in collaboration in 1965), is thin, and stands

with an athlete's slope. His hair and the frames of his glasses are thick and black; his hair looks slightly electrified. He is forty-one years old, and Komar is forty-three. When Melamid is calm, he keeps his hands in the pockets of his pants or of his tan raincoat and gestures occasionally with his elbows. When he is excited, his hands fly from his pockets and fill the air, and his face is all mobility. In the presence of a woman he considers extremely beautiful, his eyes may shutter at the overload; he looks, he turns away, he puts one arm out to break his fall, he clutches at his heart. Shock is an emotion he registers in detail: "When we first emigrated to America, in 1978, I went to Times Square and I saw the movie *Superman*. I thought it was just going to be about a big man. But when he started to *fly!* [Eyebrows shoot up.] When he made time reverse by flying so fast around the earth the other way! [Head jerks back.] My *God!* [Eyes widen.] In Russia, there is nothing like this—there is nobody . . . [Hands beseech heaven.] In Russia, we have never seen—*incredible!* [Jaw falls to chest.]"

KOMAR: Yes, and since that movie have been two more, *Superman II* and *Superman III*. So now we are in America eight years, or three Supermen.

Komar and Melamid have painted in classrooms in Moscow; in the streets of a village called Brodke, about two hundred miles from Moscow, where people stood watching them and spitting sunflower seeds; in apartments in the neighborhood of Moscow University; in a summer camp for children outside the city; in a studio in the Women's League for Israel building, on Ibn Gabirol Street, in Jerusalem, where the smell of their spray painting made the birds in the courtyard fall silent; and in an apartment on East Thirty-third Street, in New York. Today, Komar lives in that apartment, and Melamid lives with his wife of seventeen years and two children in Jersey City, and they work in a loft on Canal Street upstairs from a Chinese theatrical club. Often, they paint Stalin: Stalin by a red-draped desk smiling as he receives a book for revision from the muse of history, Stalin peering through red curtains in the back window of a limousine, Stalin seated at a red-plush-upholstered dressing table staring at himself in the mirror. Or they sculpt busts of Stalin, or paint themselves in red neckerchiefs and short pants blowing gold trumpets and saluting a bust of Stalin, or they sketch scenes in an unlikely Soviet ballet, with Mikhail Baryshnikov in a white marshal's uniform dancing the part of Stalin. (Komar: "Stalin and Baryshnikov look much alike, you know, especially in eyes and eyebrows.") Or they paint a young couple making love standing up beneath a portrait of Stalin on the day his death was announced, or they paint Ronald Reagan as a centaur, or they paint two Bolsheviks with a red flag and a lantern examining a tiny dinosaur baring its teeth at them in the snow, or they photograph themselves in togas and lighted halos

going on a descent into hell, or they make a hypo-
thetical American propaganda poster of a black man
and a white man in tuxedos standing next to each
other and smiling above the legend "Black and White,
Brothers Forever," or (lately) they make multi-
paneled works on wood or big canvases, using oil
paints, acrylics, pencil, colored inks, newspaper scraps,
aluminum bowls, New Coke bottles, working clocks,
artificial flowers, and black plastic rats. Some people
who view their work laugh out loud occasionally;
others do not. At a group show in Brooklyn several
years ago, a part-time radio-talk-show host and pro-
fessed Trotskyite slashed their full-length, life-size
portrait of Hitler, because, he said, he was "tired of
irony."

KOMAR: Alex and I met in morgue. It was at Institute
for Physical Culture, in Moscow, where we went for
anatomy drawing.

MELAMID: We were born in the same hospital, we
grew up in same neighborhood, but we met only in
art school.

KOMAR: We went to art school at the Stroganov
Institute. It was named after same guy as beef Stroganov.

MELAMID: The full, official name was the MVKhPU
(ex-Stroganov) Institute. Originally, it was named
Stroganov, after the count who founded it for teach-

ing trades of making silver and china for tsar's court, then the Bolsheviks got rid of that decadent name when they converted it to modernist design workshop, then Stalin decided to put the name back when he wanted to return to ancient patriotic traditions after the war. MVKhPU stands for something like Moscow Highest Artist Industry for Art and Design.

KOMAR: For anatomy drawing, we went on Wednesdays in evening to Institute for Physical Culture, which is for athletes and teachers of athletes, because they had a morgue with many bodies floating in formaldehyde in tanks. You see, by Marxist theory if you want to develop your muscles you have to study whole structure of body. If you wish to draw muscles, it is the same. To class often we brought bottle of good Armenian cognac.

MELAMID: It was bad cognac.

KOMAR: Alex, no, you are thinking of that bad cognac in Brighton Beach.

MELAMID: Darlink, what am I telling you? I remember that cognac and it was bad cognac. Terrible.

KOMAR: And so we would sit with other students in the dim light in between the tanks with the bodies and drink this good cognac and discuss philosophy, politics, sex, and the problems of life and death.

MELAMID: Pollock was a heavy drinker. We knew this. We wished to be like the heavy-drinking artists we admired. We came from very strict families, so much of our art education was learning to drink.

KOMAR: In Russia, just Jewish people don't drink. You can recognize them easily on the street, because they're not drunk. In art school, we became assimilated Jews.

MELAMID: In art school, we learned to drink with eating. We learned that with vodka you need a strong snack like herring to punch you back into this world.

KOMAR: Art education is free in Russia. There are just maybe five schools. Twenty people like to get for one place. Artists are one of the best-salary people in Russia, and the Union of Artists is the best well-paying union. Also, art school is the only place in Russia you could look at naked girls.

MELAMID: There were lots of models. They belonged to a union for naked models, which was part of Cultural Workers' Union. It was a union like here —seniority was important for power. So some of the models were very old. Drawing them was supposed to be good to work on big forms. They always remembered posing for famous Russian artists of twenties. Some of the models were men also, of course. Some of the girls were young and lost and trying to find what to do with their lives. By Russian standards, to pose naked it needs a lot of guts. Some were so beautiful.

KOMAR: Each day of academical drawing was four hours. About eight people working at the time. Outside was winter, dark. Inside was light, electric fireplace, everybody sweat, model with sweat. There was a lot of noise. Russian pencil makes special noise, like young pig.

MELAMID: Art school was eight hours of classes in the day, then homework. If you were a few minutes late in the morning, they would mark on a list. Some days were for drawing, some for painting, some for art history, some for sculpture. There were many statues in the institute. I had a small income by betting people that I can jump up on the head of a stone girl, or on a big head of Apollo.

KOMAR: Alex was good jumper.

MELAMID: Art school was the beginning of everything.

Summers, Komar and Melamid went to museums, tutored kids preparing for the art-school exams in August, took vacations in the country or at the Baltic or in the Crimea, painted landscapes, read, sketched, and worked at jobs they chose from lists at the Stroganov Institute. One summer, for a change, they went to a small rural village and stayed with the mother of Melamid's nurse, Shura, for a month while they made abstract paintings outdoors in the village. The village, Brodke, had dirt roads, and houses with dirt floors, and electrical service only half restored since the war. It had recently erected its first outhouse. Every morning, Shura's mother would bring them big tumblers of home-brewed beet liquor warm from the still. The villagers who spat sunflower seeds while watching them paint wondered whether their abstract pictures might represent real objects, ones as yet unseen in Brodke.

Aside from tutoring, nothing Komar and Melamid did during the summers made them any money. The idea of students earning spending money at summer jobs does not exist in Russia. Like other students, Komar and Melamid got spending money from their parents. Komar's mother is a lawyer, and his father is a retired military lawyer. Melamid's mother is a book translator, and his father (also retired) is an expert on Germany who served in many high-ranking government positions.

Komar and Melamid graduated from the Stroganov Institute in 1967. Komar did freelance work, like restoring church murals for the Department of Architecture. Melamid got a job as a stage designer in Arkhangel'sk, six hundred and twenty miles north of Moscow, near the White Sea. Komar worked part-time for the Artistic Foundation, which markets arts and crafts, and began teaching night classes in art to children. Melamid left Arkhangel'sk, came back to Moscow, and also found a teaching job. They both designed book and record jackets, freelance, and they both married. Occasionally, they worked on paintings together, and in 1967 they took part in a joint exhibition at the Blue Bird Café, which had shown non-mainstream artists since the Khrushchev era. In 1972, they both got jobs at a summer camp for the children of aircraft-industry workers, where they did decorative paintings of Lenin and youth heroes like Pavlik Morozov, the boy who loved his country so much that he turned his own father in to the police. One day, when the director of the camp was showing them around the grounds, suddenly he stopped, stamped his foot, smiled, and said, "Here he is!" Then he told them that they were standing above a big concrete bust of Stalin that had been buried there years before, and that many busts and statues of Stalin too big to destroy were buried all over the country.

The nostalgia for childhood that for people my age in America is scattered among hundreds of images, from Mamie Eisenhower to Milton Berle to Davy Crockett, is for Komar and Melamid more concentrated.

MELAMID: In our childhood time, each schoolroom, each bank, each lobby of apartment building, each barbershop had a picture or statue of Stalin. Then, one morning, he was gone—everything associated with Stalin was bad. In the summer at the camp with the buried Stalin, we suddenly realized that Stalin art isn't good art, it's not bad art, it's just art. This was a great discovery for us, like a sun came down. There were no taboos anymore.

KOMAR: This discovery was incredible, it was like a laser. Through Stalin art, we could re-create our childhood. We could paint Socialist Realism like a guy who is doing this just for his soul. After summer at the youth camp, I went back to Moscow and painted a portrait of my then wife and me holding up a child in heroic family pose like on May Day poster, and Alex did portrait of his father just like the image of Lenin on Soviet medal.

MELAMID: When we met again in the fall and saw these pictures, we decided that's it—we should work only together.

Like many other young art-school graduates, Komar and Melamid belonged to the youth section of the Moscow Union of Artists. Youth-section affiliates are candidates for full membership in the union. There are a number of unions for artists and designers in Russia, but the Moscow Union of Artists is important, because of its good government contacts (which get its artists big government commissions), and also because it controls most of the gallery space in Moscow. A tradition or rule of the Union was that it would hold a group show of the work of youth-section members at least once a year. The events in Czechoslovakia in 1968 produced a comic catchphrase among people in Moscow. "When the Czechs said they were going to have 'socialism with a human face,' everybody thought that was the funniest thing they'd ever heard," Melamid said. "We all went around saying 'with a human face,' about everything—'dinner with a human face,' 'breakfast with a human face,' 'falling in the snow with a human face.'" The events in Czechoslovakia also produced an almost complete shutdown in the world of Russian art. After the Soviet invasion, the Moscow Union of Artists stopped having group shows for its youth-section members, and official permission to exhibit new art work was just about impossible to get.

Komar and Melamid had a high-ranking friend in the union, and in 1968 he told them about one-night, invitation-only shows that the union sometimes held for young artists. Komar and Melamid applied for one of these shows, and then, like most other Russian artists, spent the following years without any public viewing of their work at all. In 1973, their friend told them that the union was at last ready to consider their application. They took their pictures in a taxi to the union building, set them up in a conference room, and then waited outside. Through the closed door they heard somebody say, "If we discuss every question like this, we'll be here all night." Finally, a union official came out and told them they would be informed of the decision by mail, and they picked up their paintings and left.

Weeks passed with no word, so they went back to the union offices. They talked to one secretary and then another, but nobody knew anything about their case. Eventually, a secretary told them to wait and she would go find out. When she returned, she told them that permission for their show had been refused. She said that, furthermore, they were now no longer members of the youth section of the Moscow Union of Artists. She told them that they had been kicked out for "distortion of Soviet reality and deviation from the principles of Socialist Realism."

In Stalin's time, this was a crime that could have sent them to Siberia. In the early thirties, people say, it was what caused all the members of the Ukrainian nationalist art movement to be shot. Melamid thinks that, in fact, since Stalin's time nobody else had ever been charged with it. (Komar disagrees.) From their friend in the union they learned that their expulsion had been the last patriotic act of the retiring director of the youth section, who was dying of cancer. Komar recalled that when they were picking up the paintings this man had asked him several questions about a work that included an image of Laika, the famous dog that was lost in a Sputnik mission in 1957. Their friend told them that the whole thing was a lot of nonsense, and that if they were quiet for a year or two and didn't make a scandal they would surely be readmitted.

By 1973, with no place else to go, artists in Moscow had started to show their work in private apartments. After Komar and Melamid were kicked out of the youth section, they set up some of their paintings in a friend's apartment, where people came on Saturdays to look and talk and drink tea and vodka. On an evening of performance art that ended when neighbors called the police, Komar and Melamid met a painter named Oscar Rabine, who was known for his

uncheerful landscapes and his Pop-art-inspired pictures of rubles. For some time, Rabine had been trying different ways to get permission for a show, and
now he had the idea of holding it outdoors. Almost
no one in Russia had ever heard of an outdoor art
show. Komar and Melamid encouraged Rabine in
this idea and told him they would join any outdoor art show he could arrange. They went with him
on one of his many trips to Moscow City Hall, where
he gave aides to Mayor Vladimir F. Promyslov a list
of possible sites. Months and months went by. The
officials Rabine met with advised him strongly against
having any outdoor show, but none would give him
a definite, written no. In September of 1974, the artists informed the City Council that they planned to
hold the show in two weeks if there were no objec-
tions. The City Council asked that the Communist
Party Committee of the Union of Artists review the
pictures; the artists brought the pictures in; an official finally told them that their exhibition would be
neither encouraged nor forbidden. Rabine typed up
and mailed invitations for a show on Sunday, September 15, at an open field in a neighborhood called
Belyayevo, on the southwestern edge of the city. Komar and Melamid invited people over the phone.

From the roof of a high-rise apartment building
near the field, Komar and Melamid checked out the
site on the evening before the show. The next morning, carrying their paintings, they went by the build-

ing for another look. Now there was a man on the roof with a movie camera aimed at the field; another man followed them from the building.

KOMAR: I did not believe government would really do something against our show. It was beginning of time of détente. In Moscow was then just open an office of Chase Manhattan Bank. Also, we invite many foreign correspondents we know. We thought because of them our show would be protect.

MELAMID: What we were doing was so legal. If the government wished to stop this show, we gave them already many opportunities.

KOMAR: Our psychological condition at the time is hard to describe. Art in Moscow was like a dead sea. We were tired of fear. Even in prison would be better.

MELAMID: This field in Belyayevo is a big, big place. No such thing in Russia exists like these cut-grass lawns in America. A drizzle was falling, so everywhere was mud.

KOMAR: Mud in Russia looks like mustard.

MELAMID: Two or three hundred people were walking everywhere on this field. We could not see other artists. We took out our pictures to show them, but right away this guy came up to us and said, "No no no! We are going to be planting trees here!"

KOMAR: At first, was no police with uniforms. Was only volunteer helpers of police. I think many was students from police academy. They all had same blue raincoat.

MELAMID: Many of these guys everywhere. Also, there was a big truck with young trees, dump trucks with soil, a truck for washing streets, and a bull-dozer—

KOMAR: At least two bulldozers, perhaps four, with Moscow city colors—yellow and blue.

MELAMID: We moved to another spot and tried again to put up our pictures. Again, these guys told us they were planting trees there, also. So again we moved. We were like robots going automatically by inertia. All day, I do not think one artist ever could show one picture.

KOMAR: This volunteer helper of police grab from me our double self-portrait as Marx and Lenin. I took neutral position: If you like my picture, have it. Then he put it on ground with his foot to broke it. I said to him, "That's not regular picture—it's masterpiece." That stopped him for a minute. He didn't want to be barbarian.

MELAMID: Then it was such a mess. People were shouting, "Help, they are beating us!" The machine for washing streets was spraying at people, they were running all over. All the trucks were making noise with their loud motors.

KOMAR: We were very lucky. They did it good for us. Without these machines, there would be no event. It was very nice—like elephants in circus.

MELAMID: Everybody was being beaten. A very nice girl from AP news, they punched her camera. A man from *The New York Times*, they chipped his tooth—

KOMAR: I was pushed down to mud. I was like Gandhi, I not resist. I saw our friend from the Union of Artists—he was there at beginning. Then he disappeared. Another friend, they put him into a car head down. First his legs was like this [two fingers straight up], then they beat him and his legs was [two fingers curled].

MELAMID: This idea to look at pictures outdoors was exciting for people. Always were coming new, new, and new people. Suddenly there was in front of me this guy—this guy with a hat. He was very close to me but didn't touch me. He pointed his finger at me and said, "There's an artist—take him!"

KOMAR: I remember you was blue and shaked.

MELAMID: My *God!* He was short guy, with him were two big guys. Where can I go? Where can I hide? I'm in the middle of a field. I ran—

KOMAR: He ran right to horizon.

MELAMID: I'm running, my glasses were in water so I couldn't see properly what I am doing, I'm looking down at my dirty feet, these professional fighters of evil chasing me—

KOMAR: They look like gangsters in American movie.

MELAMID: Finally, I ran into a crowd of people, the guys said, "Ahh—let him go," and stopped chasing.

KOMAR: One of my students came, he was bent over. He said, "Somebody kick me in stomach." I saw more of my students, and I gave them two of our pictures so they could keep for later. Then I went to Metro station and got on train.

MELAMID: I saw a bulldozer start to follow artists around to try to run over them. The driver was drunk or maybe he was just excited. I heard some pictures were put in a fire. Quickly I, too, ran to the Metro. We all met after at Rabine apartment. It was a hard decision what to do. We were all shouting. "We'll write a letter to—to the whole city of Moscow! To— to all the whole Russian people! To the, the—whole people of all the *world!*"

KOMAR: We drank many liters of vodka.

MELAMID: But this moment when he pointed— "Take him!" My God, it was a moment in my life.

The next day, a front-page headline in the *Times* read, "RUSSIANS DISRUPT MODERN ART SHOW WITH BULL-DOZERS." Five artists, including Oscar Rabine, were arrested, tried for petty hooliganism in a district court, convicted, and sentenced to fifteen-day prison terms or twenty-ruble fines, or both. A man in a trenchcoat who identified himself as a local Communist Party official explained to a Western correspondent that the exhibition was broken up because workers had volun-teered to build a "park of culture" at the site. The official gave his name as Ivan Ivanovich Ivanov. News of the show instantly filled airwaves and columns of type all around the world; people called it the Bulldozer Show. The American government sent Moscow a protest over the beating of American correspondents. Tass called the show a "cheap provocation." Norman Reid, the director of London's Tate Gallery, canceled a scheduled visit to Moscow. Gus Hall, the leader of the American Communist Party, said, "One would have to be totally naïve not to see the fine hand of the CIA in this affair." In its Russian-language broadcast heard in Moscow, the BBC commented that many Western governments would be happy to use bulldozers against modernism but only the Soviet Union actually did.

Within a few days, all the arrested artists were freed. Rabine did not pay his fine. He announced that the group would hold the same show again two weeks from the original date, on Sunday, September 29. (Melamid: "This was absolutely smart decision by Rabine. When he pronounced this words, everybody knew it was right.") The Deputy Director of the Culture Administration of the Moscow City Council said the artists could have their show Saturday the twenty-eighth. The artists said that too many people had to work on Saturdays. The city authorities agreed to Sunday. Two days before the show, they announced that only "acquaintances" of the artists would be allowed to attend. This time, the show was in Izmail-ovsky Park, on the northeastern edge of the city. Sixty-five artists showed hundreds of canvases, with no censorship. More than ten thousand people came. Parents held children aloft to see paintings over the crowds. A French diplomat called the event a Russian Woodstock. The canvases included works of Surrealism, religious symbolism, abstract art, Pop art, and psychedelic art. The poet Yevgeny Yevtushenko was there. Plainclothes police made movies of the spectators.

KOMAR: It was beautiful sunny day. I was walking around seeing friends, talking, breathing—it was fantastic day. It was day of freedom.

MELAMID: Both shows were so unusual, so outrageous in Russian life. For an hour, we lived like real Western people.

KOMAR: After, was many shows. A lot of public went to shows—in Moscow, in Leningrad, in official galleries, in apartments. Imagine—our friend saw permission letter for show with signature of Kosygin himself. Everybody else was afraid to sign. Government let artists paint and show everything but religion and pornography. But they never said they was sorry for past.

MELAMID: Bulldozer Show was something happened never before and never again. It was enormously embarrassing for government. It was most famous art show ever in Russia. It changed the society.

Boris N. Chaplin, first secretary of the Moscow district that included the Belyayevo field, was dismissed by the Communist Party in October; later, he was appointed Ambassador to North Vietnam. Certain artists, Oscar Rabine among them, were offered membership in the Moscow Union of Artists, and Alexander Glazer, a poet and art collector who often spoke for the artists, said that this was an attempt to divide the group. A painter who had done a many-headed portrait of Christ was taken to a mental hospital; another painter was evicted from his apartment; another was called up for Army Reserve duty; officials told another they would crush him like a grain of sand. In December, Alexander Glazer was arrested, and soon afterward was told he could leave the country. City authorities gave permission for a show of unofficial art at the Exhibition of Economic Achievements, but the site they offered was the Beekeeping Pavilion, which held only a few dozen people, and long lines had to wait outside in subzero weather. On the first anniversary of the Bulldozer Show, three artists, two without paintings, showed up at the Belyayevo field. The government allowed another indoor show in Moscow, and then took forty-one paintings from the walls the night before the opening. Oscar Rabine was detained, released, arrested, released again. Yevgeny Rukhin, a tall and lively painter who had been arrested at Belyayevo, died in a fire in his studio.

Alexander Goldfarb, a cousin of Melamid's who had emigrated to Israel, knew somebody who knew Ronald Feldman, a New York art dealer. Goldfarb described Komar and Melamid's work to Feldman, and he gave them a show in his gallery, on East Seventy-fourth Street, in 1976, and it was a hit. Some of the paintings were smuggled from Russia disguised as tablecloths. Early in 1977, Komar and Melamid applied for visas to leave Russia, and were then kicked out of the Graphic Artists' Organization, which they had belonged to for several years. In October, Melamid and his wife and children were allowed to emigrate to Israel; Komar, still in Moscow, said that now they would try to collaborate through telepathy. Eight weeks later, Komar was also allowed to leave. They built an aluminum temple on Mt. Zion and burned a Russian suitcase.

KOMAR: Today, every artist from Bulldozer Show is either emigrate or dead.

MELAMID: And our friends who come to visit us from Moscow tell us there are no trees growing in Belyayevo field to this day.

Komar and Melamid like New York, but they like London, Amsterdam, and Paris better. Jerusalem, where they lived less than a year, they did not like at all. Haarlem, Holland, is perhaps their favorite all-around city, and they think of moving there or to Amsterdam someday. In Paris, Komar enjoys walking under the trees on the avenues with beautiful women, and Melamid likes drinking and talking and staying up all night and getting dizzier and dizzier. As they were telling me how great Paris is, they said that a show of their pictures was opening in a week at the Musée des Arts Décoratifs there, and that they were going for a ten-day visit, and that I should come, too. To their surprise, I did.

The passport photographer in Grand Central, to get me to smile, said, "Say 'Money.'" And, in fact, when the desk clerk at my hotel showed me how to unlock the minibar in my room and I handed him a bill I picked at random from my new wad of francs he gave me the biggest smile I saw the whole time I was in France. I sat on the edge of the bed and drank a Sunshine-brand orange drink from the minibar. Then I called Komar and Melamid at the Hôtel de la Tamise, where they said they'd be staying, and Komar answered and said, "Ah. Yes." Then he and a Parisian friend, Irina Markowicz, a student of psychology at the Sorbonne, met me at the corner of the Rue de Rivoli and the Rue de l'Échelle, and Komar said he didn't know where Melamid was, and we went to a coffee shop and Irina ordered for us, and then we walked around and Komar pointed to a woman with an Alsatian that was better dressed than he and I put together and he said, "In Paris, dogs are different." Then we went into the Café des Deux Magots, and I told Komar that James Joyce supposedly used to go there and Komar said, "I remember like it was now," and then we walked by a statue of Danton and Komar said that when he was a kid much of the candy in

Russia was named after revolutionaries and he remembered especially Marat chocolates, and then we went to a restaurant for lunch and Irina said she had a friend who wouldn't drink wine no matter how good if it was served in the wrong kind of glass and I said that I sometimes drank wine from a glass from the bathroom with a little toothpaste crescent on the rim and Irina's hand fluttered to her breast and she said, "Ohhh, *horrible!*" Then Komar told Irina that he was sure Russia would one day take over all of Europe, and that having Europe would be good for Russia, and would civilize it. Then we walked around some more, and Komar said that once when he was in Novosibirsk, when he was in the Army, he lit a cigarette on the street and immediately drew a crowd of about thirty people all holding unlit cigarettes, because there was a shortage of matches in Novosibirsk at the time. Then we went looking for a café that Komar said had a bronze plaque at a table saying that Lenin used to eat there, but we couldn't find it. Then Komar left, and Irina showed me around the Pompidou Center art museum, and she asked me to explain what Thanksgiving dinner was in America, and why the American astronauts in the space shuttle had appeared on television eating it out of plastic packs, and then Irina had to go to a cello lesson, and I went to my hotel and hit the minibar, and then I went out to dinner and had rabbit stew, and then I went back to the hotel and went to sleep.

That was Thursday. For the next several days, I was kind of in shock. I had never spent more than an afternoon in a foreign country before. I thought I spoke French, but I don't. The times I called Komar and Melamid at their hotel, they were out. I sat in my hotel room and read the Paris phone book; it lists a Marcel Proust and eight Henri Rousseaus. At night, there were almost no sirens or horns, only bells on the hour. I went to see buildings where Turgenev and Hemingway and Gertrude Stein used to live, and I walked on Avenue MacMahon, named for Marshal MacMahon, a military hero of the era of Louis-Napoleon and a fifth-great-grandfather of the To-night Show's Ed McMahon.

Finally, I ran into Komar one afternoon in the Louvre. He was holding his camera sideways to pho-tograph a Le Brun drawing, and I waited until he was through and went up and said hi, and he said, "Hello, how are you doink?" I gave him a lively ac-count of the things I'd seen, and he said that I should go in a couple of hours to the gallery where their show was, because he and Melamid were meeting some French journalists there. So I left the mu-seum, and somebody said "Now, where's Mother got to?" and I did a few errands, and I went to the gal-lery. Komar and Melamid were just standing around. The journalists hadn't shown up. A hard rain fell and then stopped. So Melamid and I went to look again for the café with the Lenin plaque, and Komar said he'd meet us later at a show at the Museum of Modern

Art, and men in blue jumpsuits with long brooms were helping small pieces of trash along the flow of rainwater in the gutters, and Melamid said that New York was becoming such an impossible place to live that soon all New York artists would have to decide between moving to Paris and moving to New Jersey. I told Melamid that I thought Paris was like a girl who wouldn't go out with me in high school. Rush hour started, and Frenchmen sped past us in little cars with their knees up around their ears. We crossed the Pont Alexandre III, dedicated by Tsar Nicholas II and his wife in 1896, and Melamid said that since the Gorbachev anti-alcoholism campaign all the Soviet Russians in Paris had stopped drinking, which was spooky. The streetlights on the bridge had columns with lions' feet at the base and, above, coats of arms, and oak leaves, and cattails, and more leaves. Tangled in the wrought-iron work of one of the lights were many yards of brown vinyl audio tape, which fluttered out over the river in the wind.

We never found the café with the Lenin plaque, and when we tried to walk to the Museum of Modern Art we went a long way in the wrong direction by accident, and at a taxi stand Melamid stepped in front of a woman holding a stroller, packages, and a crying baby, and I said, "But she's got a kid," and Melamid said, "So, I've got two kids," but we let her have the taxi and we took the next one, and the museum was full of people and the smell of wine sweat and cologne, and you needed an invitation, which Melamid somehow got, and then he ran into his friends Michael Burdzelian, a Russian-émigré artist who lives in Paris, and Michael Gurvitch, a vacationing solid-state physicist who works for Bell Laboratories in New Jersey. The new works of art on display were empty picture frames hanging on a wall, and live women in funnel hats doing a minimal dance, and partly crushed automobile windshields arranged on a floor, and at each work Melamid exclaimed, "Ohhh—is pretty. Is so *pretty!*" I asked him if he was serious, and he said "What I am saying is . . ." and he notched two sets of quotation marks in the air with his fingers, and I reflected that the gesture could serve as the international hand signal for irony. We never found Komar, and on the way out Melamid stopped at a sculpture that consisted of a smashed-up grand piano, and Melamid said, "This I like." Then Michael Burdzelian, Michael Gurvitch, Melamid, and I went to a restaurant near the Pont Louis-Philippe and ordered escargots and pâté for appetizers, and the waitress turned pale and explained how the *huile* of the escargots would clash with the taste of the pâté, and when we left I gave her a ten-dollar bill and Michael Burdzelian said, "That was an enormous tip. Don't do that again." Then we took some taxis and went to some bars, and at one point we were sitting at a round table with four Polish women and a Polish folksinger in a restaurant called Anna Karenina, and one of the women told me I looked like the designer Karl Lagerfeld, which I guess was a compliment, and

Michael Gurvitch said that his theory about the novel *Anna Karenina* was that the short, grimy man muttering French who appears in Vronsky's nightmare, in Anna's nightmare, at the train station, and then just as Anna goes under the wheels is in fact Tolstoy himself, and then a Polish woman with a big black purse with about a dozen clasps and latches on it told me that when she came to New York, as she hoped she would someday, she wanted first to go up to the top of the Empire State Building and eat an omelette, and then go down into a dark underground bar and listen to an old, old black man play jazz. Finally, about three in the morning, I was walking by myself. In a silent square with black windows all around and a floodlit statue in the middle, there was a man sleeping on a flattened box on the sidewalk with his coat buttoned up to the neck. Beside him, an umbrella was neatly furled.

The next morning, I flew back to Kennedy Airport, and when the Carey bus to the city stopped at a light in Queens I saw by the curb a late-model Pontiac with its windows shattered to powder and its interior burned out and its hood up and shreds of black metal corkscrewing off all over. In Paris, the only object I saw which was as badly damaged was a piece of sculpture.

Between January of 1985 and April of 1986, Komar and Melamid made more than fifty paintings, in a

variety of styles that omitted few of the major move-
ments in the history of art. The Ronald Feldman
Gallery had a show entitled "Anarchistic Synthesism,"
featuring forty-one of these paintings—more than six-
teen hundred square feet of panel board and canvas.
So many people came to the opening that you could
not stand in any one place for long. Eyes looked at
paintings and paused and thought their thoughts and
moved on. A woman leaned against a painting for a
moment, talking. A man in a black leather jacket said
something to another man in a black leather jacket
and gestured with a pink plastic baby bottle in the
shape of a Teddy bear. A woman in a black suit
smoked with her palm upward. A man held his
glasses by one temple and swung them at a painting.
In the forest of legs, a little boy stamped to pieces one
of the plastic cups the wine was served in.

In Komar and Melamid's empty studio, the mice
now had no stacks of paintings to hide behind. When
I stopped by a couple days after the opening, they
were zipping back and forth across the floor like beams
of light. Komar has not had a drink in over a year,
so after a while just Melamid and I went to the 3
Roses Bar, on Canal Street. Melamid loves this bar.
Especially on weekdays, it is a favorite of black
people who work downtown. Occasionally, the bar is
crowded and Melamid is the only white person. Va-
nessa, the barmaid, has fingernails maybe eight inches
long on one hand, and taped to a cabinet behind her
is a photograph of them at an earlier length.

"Here I am not Russian, not immigrant, not Jewish, not famous artist," Melamid said. "Here I am just white. Or Puerto Rican, maybe. I enjoy very much the romanticism of this place—the lights of the beer advertisements, the colors of the drinks, the paper decorations. The romantic school is still alive in American bars—maybe only there. For the most part, New York City is not romantic. The surfaces are all straight, like mathematical, architectural drawing. In Moscow, the builders were not so skilled, and the lines are always a little bit crooked. Moscow— 'Москва,' the word—is feminine, and everything in Moscow has a curve or it bulges out, and I was always wanting to rub against the buildings. I believe this 3 Roses Bar exist because of the paintings of Hopper —not the other way around. In Russia, in last century, a landscape painter named Levitan invented the famous picturesque Russian countryside with churches and birch trees. Before Levitan, birch trees were invisible, and so did not exist. I do not believe Russian today would understand Komar and Melamid paintings, no. Sometimes in our work we are describing Russia to West, and this makes us very Western to Russians. Our dealer told us today that from our show we sold paintings to Sylvester Stallone and Arnold Schwarzenegger. So we are selling well to musclemen—I do not know why.

"All my life, I try to be free. I do not feel freer in America—I have a family, responsibilities. These are more burdensome to the world than any state. Last

year, I crashed my car, and I was so happy. I said, 'I
don't need a car.' But I live in New Jersey, so of course
I had to get another one. When Vitaly and I first
came here, we discovered that American artists can
make for themselves the most unfree situations. Many
times they are creating stylistic solitary confinements.
A man paints one line on a canvas for his whole life
and it is an unthinkable decision to make it across
instead of up-and-down. In this New York art business, we are on a conveyor belt—shows, paintings,
sales, galleries. I'm a bum by definition. At least once
a year, I must sleep in my dress—my clothes. I'm
afraid every day that something will stop me from
painting and then I'll be real bum. The best descrip-
tion of an artist is he was born in this year and he
died in this year. We do not think ahead when we
paint. We spend no more than one day on a picture.
Splash one, splash another, put straight lines. You
must work every day and work everything you can do.
We paint in styles, yes, like Stone Age man or Botticelli or Jasper Johns or whoever, but really it is because we *are* Botticelli. We are a cocktail of all artists
who have lived. This is our greatest discovery: according to Marxist theory, there is on one side the enormous, powerful force of history and on the other side
the helpless, tiny individual. What we discover is that
there is no difference between the two. The individual is the history of the world, the history of art. At a
show at the Palazzo Vecchio, in Florence, several years
ago, Vitaly and I saw a show of watercolors by Hitler

—cityscapes, mostly, which I thought were bad and Vitaly thought were not so bad. Hitler was rejected from art school for these pictures, so he went on to make real city ruins. Somebody, I forget who, once said that all artists are unsuccessful dictators, and vice versa. When I paint, I see I have Hitler in me."